THE LULU PLAYS
THE MARQUIS OF KEITH

Contents

Introduction

Frank Wedekind's work and life were inextricably mixed. In the first of *The Lulu Plays, Earth Spirit,* the character Alva is writing a play called *Earth Spirit* in which, as Rodrigo says 'my fiancée's legs are the two central characters'. Indeed, the extent of Alva's success as a playwright closely reflects Wedekind's own at the time *Earth Spirit* was written. Similarly he said of his hero, the Marquis of Keith, 'It's me, as I seemed to myself at thirty-five in relation to the theatre and society.'

Wedekind (full name Benjamin Franklin Wedekind) was the son of a radical doctor who had travelled widely in Europe before meeting his much younger wife Emilie (at the time earning her living as a singer) in San Francisco. The couple returned to Germany where Frank, one of five brothers and sisters, was born in 1864.

Early in life Wedekind developed a view of the world as far outside normal conventions as his parents' lifestyle. Open conflict is said to have been the preferred means of clearing the air in the Wedekind household, and a sister later asserted that rows she'd had with her brother appeared wholesale in his play *The Concert Singer.*

His father's belief and experience (as a political activist) was that all efforts towards idealistic goals must be predicated upon material independence (see The Marquis of Keith's advice to Hermann in Act One). If Frank rejected this view, he would have to make his own way in life without his father's financial help. The young Frank left home suddenly, provoked by a slighting remark about his mother, and worked as a journalist for a year until reconciliation with his father shortly before his death.

Out of sympathy with the prevailing Naturalism of his day, Wedekind's early stage work demonstrated the naivety of the young provincial enthusiast for the arts, but without that seasoned insight into the market forces of showbiz which was to characterise his later work. It also announced his early denunciation of 'sympathy' for the working class as just another form of condescension. He felt it achieved little more than the well-being of the 'sympathiser' and ignored the vital energy and self-awareness of those who refuse to be debased by misplaced philanthropy.

He was also concerned to show abstract idealism as potentially destructive of human relationships, particularly where it infringes upon an individual's right to self-determination. Thus, while championing women's emancipation, he was also aware of the loss to the self-determining woman of what he saw as the main advantage to women of an otherwise cossetting bourgeois marriage – the freedom to give and receive love.

Spring Awakening, though completed by Easter 1891, was not premiered until November 1906. Heavily censored, friends could not understand why at the time he disavowed Frau Gabor's open method of education which he is said to have drawn from aspects of his own mother. (The play subsequently remained in Reinhardt's repertoire for 615 performances over twenty years.)

Always short of money, an inheritance from his father allowed him to live in Paris for four years (with a six-month visit to London), during which time he frequented the café society of painters and musicians where it was not uncommon to pay for one's daily bread with a painting (as Keith does with his 'Saranieffs'). During this time he first worked on *The Lulu Plays*. These were published in a number of different forms – partly due to censorship problems – and were subject to confiscation before production in 1898, with Wedekind himself playing Dr Schoen. The audience was recruited from trade union and workers education association members.

Social standing and success never counted for much in his assessment of those around him. In Paris he got to know Willy Gretor, who embodied (in Wedekind's terminology) 'Mr Lickety-Split' and became the model for the Marquis of Keith. Gretor was a successful painter (though more successful as a dealer) and was gifted with that 'brutal intelligence of the predator' which he so admired in Steinruck's portrayal of Dr Schoen.

In spite of repeated, spectacular flops in Munich, his work was constantly premiered at the Schauspielhaus. He completed *The Marquis Of Keith* in the last year of the century but actually saw the twentieth century in, sitting in prison for his socially satirical poems in the magazine *Simplicissimus*. He later considered it his 'artistically most mature and intellectually richest' play, and the Marquis as the best role he ever wrote.

> ...with his curious posture, slightly stooped but with his close-cropped importunate skull jutting forward... He stood there, ugly, brutal, dangerous, his red hair crew-cut, his hands in his pockets, and you had the feeling not even the devil could move him.
>
> – Brecht on Wedekind as the Marquis of Keith

Although now respected by his peers, 'My royalties are still not at that level where I can move freely. One hopes and hopes and hopes from one flop to the next, from one apparent success to the next. Four years ago...was the change in my fortunes, but how slow the road upwards has been. I would never have dreamt it possible.' The productions in which Wedekind himself appeared were more successful than those in which professionals appeared alone.

On 1 May 1906 he married the just twenty year-old Tilly Newes. On 2 May they appeared together as Casti-Piani and Lisiska in his one-acter *Damnation*. Friends gave them a maximum of ten years together and one warned Tilly, 'Watch out. From now on he'll try to make you drop everything he's liked about you so far.' He was able to suppress the jealousy Tilly rightly suspected he'd inherited from his father only for a short while. Even so, the values one would anticipate from his plays – *Spring Awakening* in particular – appear to have been carried out scrupulously with his own children:

> ...he was always extremely polite and took our answers seriously, and in consequence we always tried to live up to the demands he made on our attentiveness and understanding. He treated us like equals. But what I

liked best was the trouble he took to be happy and, even when fatally ill, to leave us children feeling happy... You never felt inferior to him because you were small and weak and ignorant. The certain knowledge that anyone who abuses power can't be worth much has remained with me ever since.

– Wedekind's daughter, Kadidja

He had also found in Tilly a Lulu with whom he could counter the legendary Gertrud Eysoldt's portrayal, itself a riposte to the ultra-naturalistic concept of Lulu as a man-eating flirt. But the portrayal of Lulu as a sophisticated vamp was equally hard to dispel – this was the type of woman, Wedekind commented, men run a mile from. An amoral Lulu, free of value judgement was still difficult to achieve, though guest appearances by the Wedekinds offered a model of 'matter-of-fact-ness' in the interpretation of the plays, along with pace, passion and wit – equally differentiated from the pathos of the Court Theatre as from naturalistic 'under-acting'.

In his last play *Simson* he anticipated the sense of helplessness and being at others' mercy which accompanied his own death from the complications of an operation for appendicitis at the age of fifty-four. The following descriptions of his funeral give some idea of the impact he had finally made:

At the cemetery there had collected around the catafalque not only Wedekind's friends and acquaintances...but also an assortment of street-life, above all prostitute women and girls, hoping to pay their last respects... As the procession set off, this crowd of unwelcome garecrashers welled forward and, overtaking each other ahead of the coffin, rushed to be first by the grave so as not to miss any of the show...

– Kurt Martens

...a motley swarm of dubious girls, and adolescent boys pressed forward and sprinted from the chapel, off over graves and memorials, to the open grave like nothing more than a herd of insane deer... As the casket was lowered Lautensack interrupted the calm which had been restored by throwing a huge bouquet of red roses down, falling to his knees, reaching wildly into the pit and crying out 'To Frank Wedekind, my reacher, my idol, my mentor – from your unworthy pupil.' People were horrified.

– Otto Falckenberg

For me, the approach from Jonathan Holloway of Red Shift to do a new adaptation of *The Lulu Plays* came at a time when I was keen to return to translating, having completed several original plays for production in the preceding eighteen months. The challenge of adapting *Earth Spirit* and *Pandora's Box* into one two-hour show (to fit into an Edinburgh Festival 'time-slot') and for only seven actors (for the now all-too-familiar reasons of finance) was one I relished. My experience both in writing for small-scale touring theatre and also as a Literary Editor in theatres told me that, with luck, the plays would benefit – certainly in their profile in the English-speaking theatre. Indeed, it seems that at least one of the versions *The Lulu Plays* went through envisaged a similar collapsing of Lulu's whole story into one play.

An obvious target for the red pencil was the exposition in *Pandora's Box* of much that has happened in *Earth Spirit.* But turn-of-the-century German theatre was in any case more tolerant of exposition and repetition than English theatre today, so all story-telling which merely reinforced what was evident from the action had to go. We were also forced to lose minor characters (like Hugenberg and Escerny), but in striking them out, the lines of Lulu's development emerged more clearly. So neat were the excisions in fact, that only one or two invented lines have been necessary to bridge the resulting gaps. Finally, Wedekind's lifelong fascination with (and still pertinent insight into) the process of arts production seemed sadly to hold up the dramatic advance of the play from time to time, so much of that had to go too.

A read-through of an early draft came in at just under two hours. But it revealed (along with some very apposite questions from actors in auditions) that occasional lines of what had seemed murky exposition actually gave vital – though frequently ambiguous – clues to characters' past history and present motivation. These lines went back in, and what appears here now is basically a cut version with, I trust, the best of Wedekind and all the material necessary for an informed production still intact.

Having enjoyed the work on *Lulu* so much, I was delighted when the Gate Theatre at Notting Hill also expressed interest in *The Marquis Of Keith*. This play was something of a rediscovery for me, having first read it as a student of German many years before. Most striking was its contemporary relevance to the 1980s – a wheeler-dealer hero in a world populated by penurious artists on the one hand and the cynical rich on the other.

The other revelation – thanks to a reading by students at Central School of Speech and Drama – was the play's humour. This is not a quality associated in the Anglo-Saxon mind with German culture; but a poor and academic tradition of translation must take some of the blame for this.

Unlike with *Lulu*, there was no practical need to cut heavily. A slight sub-plot with Simba's boyfriend, and some bit parts in the third act party had to go purely because it is uneconomic in present conditions to engage actors in such tiny parts. The other consideration was where to put the interval. The best place seemed after the party, but this meant that a first half of the full three acts would be rather long. As this was the part of the play where most of the expositional lines and some familiar Wedekind philosophising occurred, it is where most of the 'nipping and tucking' was done.

Finally, in reading around Wedekind's life and work, I discovered a couple of quotes from the man himself which I trust will be useful pointers to future producers of these extraordinary plays:

I have never put my own convictions in the mouths of my characters. It would be too stupid anyway, to have them come to grief through, of all things, their opinions. My own views are expressed through the balance-sheet thrown up at the end of the play by the way the action has gone and the fate of the principal characters.

I know no one you could describe simply as a sinner. For even the best qualities are testimony to an educated, and therefore, refined and more cunning, form of egotism.

– Frank Wedekind

Steve Gooch, 1990

THE LULU PLAYS

EARTH SPIRIT
PANDORA'S BOX

Act One, 'Earth Spirit', takes place in Germany.
Act Two, 'Pandora's Box', Scene 1 takes place in Germany,
Scene 2 takes place in Paris, Scene 3 takes place in London.

Characters

DR SCHOEN
a chief editor

ALVA
his son, a writer

SCHWARZ
a painter

DR GOLL
a chief health officer

LULU

SCHIGOLCH

RODRIGO
an artiste

COUNTESS GESCHWITZ
a painter

FERDINAND
a coachman

MARQUIS CASTI-PIANI

BIANETTA

BOB
a hotel boy

HUNIDEI

KUNGU POTI
an African Prince

JACK

May be played with seven actors.

This adaptation of *Lulu* was commissioned by Red Shift Theatre Company and received its première at the Edinburgh Festival in 1990, with the following cast:

ALVA, Robin Brooks

DR SCHOEN / CASTI-PIANI / JACK, Carl Forgione

COUNTESS GESCHWITZ, Janet Jeffries

LULU, Clara Salaman

SCHIGOLCH, Jeremy Wilkin

DR GOLL / BIANETTA / BOB / FERDINAND / HUNIDEI, David Young

SCHWARZ / RODRIGO / KUNGU-POTI, Igor Thompson

This commission was made possible by Battersea Arts Centre.

ACT ONE
Earth Spirit

Scene 1

A spacious studio. Door to the street up right. Door to the bedroom down right. A podium in the middle. A folding screen behind the podium. A Turkish carpet in front of it. Two easels down left. On the upstage one, the bust of a young girl. A canvas leans against the downstage one, turned inwards. In front of the easels, towards centre stage, an ottoman, over which is a tiger skin. Two armchairs against the wall, right. A stepladder in the background. SCHOEN is sitting on the end of the ottoman, scrutinising the bust on the upstage easel. SCHWARZ beside him, palette and brushes in hand, steps back.

SCHWARZ: The colour's sunk back a bit.

SCHOEN: (*Scrutinising him.*) Have you ever actually loved a woman?

SCHWARZ: You still don't feel there's a living body beneath the clothing.

SCHOEN: I'm sure it'll turn out well.

SCHWARZ: If you come over this way...

SCHOEN: (*Stepping back, knocks the downstage canvas over.*) Oh, sorry. (*SCHWARZ picks the canvas up. SCHOEN is struck by it.*) What's this?

SCHWARZ: D'you know her?

SCHOEN: No. (*SCHWARZ puts the picture on the easel. We see a woman dressed as a pierrot with a tall shepherd's crook in her hand.*) You've got her well.

SCHWARZ: You know her?

SCHOEN: No.

SCHWARZ: It isn't finished yet.

SCHOEN: Ah well.

SCHWARZ: What can I do? While she sits for me, I have the pleasure of entertaining her ageing husband. – We talk about art of course. Just to complete my happiness.

SCHOEN: And the old man stands guard?

SCHWARZ: It makes my blood boil.

SCHOEN: One can tell from the picture.

SCHWARZ: She never opens her mouth. – Let me show you the costume.
(*Gets it.*)

SCHOEN: (*Downstage.*) Still rather young for his age...

SCHWARZ: (*Showing him the costume.*) What is this material?

SCHOEN: Satin. – How on earth's she get in it?

SCHWARZ: I've no idea. (*As SCHOEN examines the legs.*) She rolls the left leg up.

SCHOEN: In see-through stockings?

SCHWARZ: And such a flirt with it.

SCHOEN: What gives you that dreadful idea?

SCHWARZ: Things they don't teach you in school. Things you never dreamed of. (*Looks at his watch.*) If you'd like to meet her –

SCHOEN: No.

SCHWARZ: They'll be here any minute.

SCHOEN: How much longer will the lady need to sit?

SCHWARZ: I can see my torture lasting another three months at least.

SCHOEN: I meant my lady.

SCHWARZ: Oh, sorry. Three more visits at most.
(*Accompanying him to the door.*) If Madam could leave her bodice with me perhaps...

SCHOEN: Of course. You must come and see us soon.
(*Bumps into Dr GOLL and LULU on their way in.*) Good Lord!

SCHWARZ: May I introduce –

GOLL: (*To SCHOEN.*) What on earth are you doing here?

SCHOEN: (*Kissing LULU's hand.*) Madam.

LULU: You're leaving already?

SCHOEN: I only came to see my fiancée's portrait.

LULU: (*In front of it.*) Look at this! Enchanting! So this is 'the sweet, wonderful child who's made a new man of you'.

GOLL: And you tell no one about her?

LULU: (*Turning.*) Is she always so earnest? – You really shouldn't keep her waiting any longer.

SCHOEN: I think I'll be announcing our engagement in a fortnight.

GOLL: (*To LULU.*) Come on, let's not waste time. – Hup!

LULU: Now it's my turn.

GOLL: Our Leonardo is already licking his brushes.

LULU: I imagined this far more amusing.

SCHOEN: Instead you have the satisfaction of giving us the most exquisite pleasure.

LULU: (*Moving to the door right.*) Just wait and see.

SCHWARZ: (*By the bedroom door.*) If Madam will be so kind. (*Shuts the door behind her and stands in front of it.*)

GOLL: I called her Nelli on our marriage certificate.

SCHOEN: Really.

GOLL: What d'you think?

SCHOEN: Why not call her Mignon?

GOLL: That's rather good. I didn't think of that.

SCHOEN: D'you really think the name matters so much?

GOLL: Well, you know…I haven't any children.

SCHOEN: (*Taking a cigarette case out.*) You've only been married a couple of months.

GOLL: (*Taking one.*) One is quite enough. *(To SCHWARZ.)* By the way, how's that little dancer of yours?

SCHOEN: (*Turning to SCHWARZ*) A dancer eh!

SCHWARZ: The lady sat for me as a favour, that's all.

GOLL: (*To SCHOEN.*) Ahem. – Looks like the weather's on the turn.

SCHOEN: I suppose she takes her time changing.

GOLL: Quick as lightning. A woman should be good at what she does – unless she wants to end up depending on charity. (*Calls.*) Chop-chop, Nelli!

LULU: (*Off.*) I'm coming, I'm coming.

GOLL: (*To SCHOEN.*) I don't understand these chappies. Queer fish.

SCHOEN: I envy them. They consider themselves richer than us on thirty thousand a year. You ought to become his patron.

LULU: (*Stepping out of the bedroom in a white satin pierrot costume with the left leg half-rolled up over a see-through stocking.*) Here I am. (*Coming closer.*) What d'you think?

SCHOEN: Enough to strike despair in any artist's heart.

GOLL: Don't you think?

SCHOEN: (*To LULU.*) And you're quite unaware of your effect no doubt.

LULU: I'm perfectly aware, thank you.

SCHOEN: Then you should be more discreet.

GOLL: Her skin has a whiteness I've never seen. I told our Raphael here he shouldn't waste his time on flesh-tones. I can't really get worked up about all this modern daubery.

SCHOEN: (*Anticipating SCHWARZ's response.*) Now please, let's not get too excited.

(*LULU flings her arms round GOLL and kisses him.*)

GOLL: I can see your chemise. Pull it down.

LULU: I'd as soon leave it off altogether. It only irritates.

GOLL: He ought to be up to painting it out.

LULU: (*Goes to the screen, picks up the crook and ascends the podium. To SCHOEN.*) What would you say if you had to stand on show for two hours?

GOLL: (*Sitting, right.*) Come over here.

LULU: (*Rolling up her left trouser-leg to the knee.*) How's this?

SCHWARZ: Yes...

LULU: (*A bit further.*) Like this?

SCHWARZ: Yes, yes...

GOLL: (*To SCHOEN, who has sat in the chair next to him, gesturing.*) I find I get the best angle from here.

LULU: (*Without moving.*) I beg your pardon! I'm just as good from any angle.

SCHWARZ: Right knee forward, please.

LULU: (*Raising her head.*) Paint my lips slightly apart. (*She opens her mouth slightly.*) Like this...see?

GOLL: (*To LULU.*) You should pose as if Velasquez here wasn't in the room, you know.

LULU: A painter isn't a man anyway.

SCHOEN: (*To GOLL.*) I've been meaning to ask you – have you seen that O'Morphi girl as a Peruvian pearl-diver?

GOLL: I'm going again tomorrow. My fourth time.

LULU: I think someone knocked.

SCHWARZ: Excuse me a moment.

(*Goes and opens the door.*)

GOLL: You don't have to worry about smiling at him properly, you know.

SCHOEN: I don't think he'd notice the difference.

GOLL: That's what you think! Why d'you think we're sitting here!

ALVA: (*Still behind the screen.*) May one come in?

SCHOEN: My boy!

ALVA: (*Stepping forward and shaking hands with SCHOEN and GOLL.*) Herr Doktor... (*Turning to LULU.*) What's all this! If only you could be my leading lady!

SCHOEN: What brings you here?

ALVA: I want you to see our dress rehearsal.
    (*SCHOEN rises.*)

GOLL: Have you got 'em dancing in costume already?

ALVA: Of course. Come with us. I have to be on stage in five minutes. (*To LULU.*) Sadly! (*To GOLL.*) Corticelli dances the young Buddha like she was actually born on the Ganges! D'you want to see her?

GOLL: Thanks all the same.

ALVA: Join us.

GOLL: Not on, I'm afraid.

ALVA: We're going on to Peter's afterwards. You can tell us how wonderful it was.

GOLL: You mustn't press me. Please.

ALVA: You can see the tame monkeys. The two Brahmins. The little girls...

GOLL: Can't you keep your little girls to yourself for God's sake!

LULU: Will you save us a box for Monday, Alva?

ALVA: Do I ever do otherwise?

GOLL: By the time I get back, this infernal Breughel here will have botched the picture up completely.

ALVA: That mightn't be so bad. You could have it painted over.

SCHOEN: Personally, I think your fears are unjustified.

GOLL: No, next time, gentlemen.

ALVA: The Brahmins are getting impatient. Nirvana's Daughters will be shivering in their tights.

GOLL: I'll be back in five minutes.

(*Goes down left behind SCHWARZ and compares the picture to LULU.*)

ALVA: (*To LULU.*) Alas, duty calls, Madam.

GOLL: (*To SCHWARZ.*) This needs filling out a bit here. The hair's all wrong. You're not into your subject enough...

ALVA: Come on.

SCHOEN: (*Following ALVA and GOLL.*) We'll take my cab. It's downstairs.

SCHWARZ: (*Bends over left and spits.*) Scum! It makes my pride as an artist squirm. (*After a glance at LULU.*) This is 'society'? (*Rises, goes up right, observes LULU from all sides, sits at his easel again.*) May I suggest the Chief Health Officer's wife hold her right hand a little higher?

LULU: (*Raising the crook as high as she can, to herself.*) Well who'd have thought it!

SCHWARZ: You think I'm pitiful, right?

LULU: He'll be back any minute.

SCHWARZ: All I can do is paint.

LULU: Here he is.

SCHWARZ: (*Rising.*) What?

LULU: Didn't you hear?

SCHWARZ: It's the caretaker. Sweeping the stairs.

LULU: Thank God.

SCHWARZ: D'you accompany the doctor on his visits as well?

LULU: That's all I'd need.

SCHWARZ: I meant...since you're not used to being left on your own.

LULU: We have a housekeeper at home.

SCHWARZ: Is she company for you?

LULU: She's got good taste.

SCHWARZ: In what?

LULU: She dresses me.

SCHWARZ: I suppose you're always going to balls and so on.

LULU: Never.

SCHWARZ: Why d'you need to dress then?

LULU: For my dancing.

SCHWARZ: You dance? Really?

LULU: Csárdás, Samaqueca, Skirtdance...

SCHWARZ: Who's your teacher?

LULU: He is.

SCHWARZ: Who?

LULU: He plays violin.

SCHWARZ: Well, you live and learn.

LULU: I learnt in Paris, I took classes with Eugenie
Fougere. She even let me copy her costumes.

SCHWARZ: Tell me about them.

LULU: A little green lace skirt to the knee, *décolleté* with
flounces of course, in fact very *décolleté* and very tight
round the waist −

SCHWARZ: This is too much...

LULU: Don't stop painting!

SCHWARZ: (*Scraping his spatula.*) Aren't you cold?

LULU: Heavens, no. What makes you say that? Are you?

SCHWARZ: Not today. No.

LULU: Thank God we can breathe.

SCHWARZ: What d'you mean? (*LULU breathes in deeply.*)
Stop that. Please! (*Jumps up, throws palette and brush away,
paces up and down.*) What made the man so damn keen on
a rehearsal!

LULU: I'd have sooner he stayed as well.

SCHWARZ: We really are martyrs to our profession!

LULU: I didn't mean to offend you.

SCHWARZ: (*Hesitant.*) If you could just...your left trouser-
leg...a little higher...

LULU: Like this?

SCHWARZ: (*Approaches the podium.*) If you'll allow me...

LULU: What are you doing!

SCHWARZ: I'll show you.

LULU: You mustn't.

SCHWARZ: You're nervous, that's all...
(*Tries to grab her hand.*)

LULU: (*Throws the crook in his face.*) Leave me alone!
(*Hurries to the front door.*) You wouldn't get me in a
million years.

SCHWARZ: Can't you see I was joking?

LULU: I see everything. You won't get anywhere by force. You've got no right molesting me. Get back to your easel.

(*Flees behind the ottoman.*)

SCHWARZ: (*Tries to get round the ottoman.*) As soon as I've made you pay for your flightiness.

LULU: (*Dodging.*) You'll have to catch me first.

SCHWARZ: (*Throwing himself bodily over the ottoman.*) Got you!

LULU: (*Throwing the tiger skin over his head.*) Night-night! (*Skips across the podium and climbs the stepladder.*) I can see out over all the cities of the world...

SCHWARZ: (*Disentangling himself.*) Little minx.

LULU: I can reach to the sky and stick the stars in my hair.

SCHWARZ: (*Clambering after her.*) I'll shake you off it.

LULU: Don't touch my legs! (*Topples the ladder, jumps on to the podium and, as SCHWARZ picks himself up, brings the screen down around his head. Then skips downstage to the easels.*) I said you wouldn't get me.

SCHWARZ: Let's make up. (*Tries to embrace her. LULU pushes the easel with the bust at him, bringing both crashing to the floor. SCHWARZ screams.*) My God! I'm ruined! Ten weeks' work. My trip. My exhibition. – I've got nothing to lose now.

(*Rushes after her.*)

LULU: (*Jumps over the ottoman and the fallen ladder, across the podium, then puts her foot through the portrait.*) She made a new man of him!

(*She falls forward.*)

SCHWARZ: (*Stumbling over the screen.*) Don't expect any mercy.

LULU: Leave me alone...I feel faint. Oh God. God. (*Comes downstage and collapses on the ottoman. SCHWARZ bolts the door and immediately sits beside her, clutches her hand and covers her with kisses, then stops. He is visibly struggling with an inner urge. LULU opens her eyes.*) He might come back.

SCHWARZ: I love you, Nelli.

LULU: My name isn't Nelli. (*SCHWARZ kisses her.*) It's Lulu.

SCHWARZ: I'll call you Eve.

LULU: D'you know what time it is?

SCHWARZ: (*Glances at the clock.*) Half past ten. (*LULU takes the clock and opens its case.*) You don't love me.

LULU: Don't say that...it's five past half past ten.

SCHWARZ: Kiss me, Eve.

LULU: (*Takes him by the chin and kisses him.*) You smell of tobacco.

SCHWARZ: You're fooling with me.

LULU: I'd say you were fooling yourself. – Why d'you think I'm fooling? – I've never needed to.

SCHWARZ: (*Rises, bewildered, runs his hand across his forehead.*) My God! I'm so ignorant...

LULU: (*Shrieks.*) You won't kill me, will you?

SCHWARZ: (*Turning quickly.*) You've never made love...

LULU: (*Getting half up.*) It's you've never made love!

GOLL: (*Outside.*) Open up!

LULU: (*Jumps up.*) Hide me! For God's sake, hide me!

GOLL: (*Hammering on the door.*) Open up!

(*SCHWARZ goes to open the door.*)

LULU: (*Holding him back.*) He'll kill me.

GOLL: (*Hammering on the door.*) Open up!

LULU: (*Slumps before SCHWARZ, clutching his knee.*) He'll kill me, he'll kill me.

SCHWARZ: Get up. (*The door crashes into the room. GOLL, his eyes blood-shot, staggers towards SCHWARZ and LULU, his stick raised, gasps, struggles for breath a few seconds, then crashes face down on the floor. SCHWARZ's knees wobble. LULU has fled to the door. Pause. SCHWARZ steps up to GOLL.*) Herr D – ...Herr Dok – ...Herr Doktor.

LULU: (*By the door.*) Please...tidy up the studio first.

SCHWARZ: Help me put him on the ottoman.

LULU: (*Backs away, afraid.*) No, no...

SCHWARZ: (*Tries to turn him.*) Herr Doktor.

LULU: He can't hear you.

SCHWARZ: Help me for goodness sake!

LULU: We wouldn't lift him – even together.

SCHWARZ: (*Getting up.*) We must send for a doctor.

27

(*Getting his hat.*) Please, would you mind tidying up a bit while I'm gone?
(*Goes.*)

LULU: (*Urgent.*) Sweetie! – He can't hear a thing. (*Comes downstage in a wide arc.*) He's looking at my feet, watching every step I take. His eyes follow me everywhere. (*She touches him with the end of her foot.*) Sweetie! (*Shrinks back.*) He's not kidding… No more dancing… He's left me flat. – What'll I do?
(*Crouches to the ground.*)

SCHWARZ: (*Returning.*) Still not come round?

LULU: (*Down left.*) What'll I do?

SCHWARZ: (*Bent over GOLL.*) Herr Doktor.

LULU: I don't think he's kidding.

SCHWARZ: Can't you hold a civil tongue!

LULU: He wouldn't talk to me like that. He has me dance for him when he's not feeling well.

SCHWARZ: The doctor should be here any minute.

LULU: He's beyond medicine. – Anyway, he doesn't believe in it.

SCHWARZ: Couldn't you at least get dressed?

LULU: Yes. – In a minute.

SCHWARZ: What are you waiting for?

LULU: Close his eyes.

SCHWARZ: Doesn't any of this affect you?

LULU: It'll happen to me too one day… You as well…
(*Right of GOLL.*) He's watching me.

SCHWARZ: (*Left of GOLL.*) Me too.

LULU: You're afraid!

SCHWARZ: (*Closing GOLL's eyes with a handkerchief.*) I've never had to do this sort of thing before.

LULU: Not even for your mother?

SCHWARZ: (*Nervous.*) No.

LULU: You were away?

SCHWARZ: (*Violent.*) No!

LULU: (*Recoiling.*) I didn't mean to insult you.

SCHWARZ: She's still alive.

LULU: So you've still got someone.

SCHWARZ: Poor as a church mouse.

LULU: I know what you mean.

SCHWARZ: Stop making fun of me!

LULU: I'll be rich now...

SCHWARZ: It makes your flesh creep. (*Turns away left.*) It's not her fault! (*To himself.*) She's run totally wild.

(*SCHWARZ on one side, LULU on the other, they look at each other with mistrust. SCHWARZ goes to her and takes her hand. Leads her to the ottoman, motions her to sit beside him.*) Look me in the eye.

LULU: I have to get changed.

SCHWARZ: (*Holding her back.*) One question.

LULU: I don't have to answer.

SCHWARZ: Will you tell the truth?

LULU: I don't know.

SCHWARZ: D'you believe in a creator?

LULU: I don't know.

SCHWARZ: What can you swear by?

LULU: I don't know. Let me go. You're mad.

SCHWARZ: Have you ever loved?

LULU: I don't know.

SCHWARZ: (*To himself.*) She doesn't know... He knows!

LULU: What d'you want to know?

SCHWARZ: (*Outraged.*) Get dressed! (*LULU goes into the bedroom.*) I'd gladly swop with you, corpse. Take her back. I've neither the courage nor the faith. I've had to be patient too long. It's come too late. I'm not up to happiness. – Wake up! I never touched her. Wake up! (*Kneels down and ties his handkerchief round GOLL's head.*) I hereby pray to heaven he'll give me the strength and freedom of will to be just a little happy. For her sake, only for her sake.

(*LULU comes out of the bedroom, fully clothed, her hat on, her right hand under her left armpit.*)

LULU: (*Raising her left arm.*) Could you do me up? My hand's shaking.

Scene 2

An elegant drawing-room. Up right, the main entrance. Curtained doorways down left and right. A few steps up to the doorway left. On the rear wall above the fireplace Lulu's picture as a pierrot framed splendidly in brocade. A tall mirror to the left, in front of which is a chaise-longue. To the right, an ebony writing-desk. Stage centre several armchairs around a small Chinese table. LULU, in a green silk morning gown, stands motionless in front of the mirror, wrinkles her brow, then passes her hand over it, feels her cheeks, pulls away from the mirror with a discontented, half angry glance, goes right, turning several times, opens a casket on the writing-desk, lights a cigarette, searches among the books lying on the table, picks one up, lies on the chaise-longue opposite the mirror then, after a moment's reading, lets the book sink, nods to herself earnestly and resumes her reading. SCHWARZ, palette and brush in hand, enters from the right, bends over LULU, kisses her on the forehead, goes up the steps left and turns in the doorway.

SCHWARZ: Eve!

LULU: (*Smiling.*) You called?

SCHWARZ: You look especially lovely this morning.

LULU: (*Glancing at the mirror.*) That depends on your expectations.

SCHWARZ: (*Approaching her.*) I've got a hell of a lot on today.

LULU: You're just trying to persuade yourself.

SCHWARZ: (*Puts palette and brush down and sits on the edge of the chaise-longue.*) Tell me what you dreamed last night.

LULU: That's the second time you've asked me.

SCHWARZ: (*Gets up, remembering letters in his pocket.*) News always makes me tremble. Every day I fear our world might come to an end. (*Returns to the chaise-longue, offers LULU some letters.*) For you.

LULU: (*Sniffs a letter.*) From La Corticelli. (*Tucks it in her bosom.*)

SCHWARZ: (*Flitting through a letter.*) My Samaqueca Dancer's been sold. For 50,000 Marks!

LULU: Who's that from?

SCHWARZ: Sedelmejer in Paris. That's the third picture since we got married.

LULU: (*Reads.*) Government Advisor Heinrich Riner von Zarnjkov is honoured to announce the engagement of his daughter Charlotte Marie Adelaide to Doktor Ludwig Schoen.

SCHWARZ: (*Opening another letter.*) Well at last! It seems like he's been working up to this engagement for ever. I don't understand – a man of his influence and power – what on earth could stand in his way!

LULU: What have you got there?

SCHWARZ: An invitation to take part in an international exhibition in St Petersburg. – I've no idea what to do for it.

LULU: Another enchanting girl of course.

SCHWARZ: Provided you model for me.

LULU: God knows there are enough pretty girls around.

SCHWARZ: I must get on. (*Picks up brush and palette and kisses her.*) Every day it's as if I were seeing you for the first time.

LULU: You're terrible.

SCHWARZ: (*Drops to his knees in front of the chaise-longue and caresses her hand.*) It's your fault.

LULU: (*Stroking his hair.*) You're not making the most of me. (*The doorbell rings.*)

SCHWARZ: (*Starting.*) Damn.

LULU: We're not in!

SCHWARZ: It might be my dealer. – I won't be a moment. (*Goes.*)

LULU: (*As if seeing a vision.*) Could it be you? You...? (*Closes her eyes.*)

SCHWARZ: (*Coming back.*) A beggar. Says he was in the war. I haven't got any change. (*Picks up his palette and brush.*) It's also high time I made a start.
(*He goes off left. LULU checks herself in the mirror, strokes her hair back and goes out. She comes back, leading in SCHIGOLCH.*)

SCHIGOLCH: I imagined him a bit more cavalier. More of an aura. He's a bit self-conscious. Almost passed out when he saw me standing there.

31

LULU: (*Pulling him up a chair.*) How could you ask him for money?

SCHIGOLCH: Seventy-seven years of hard practice. You told me he stuck to painting in the mornings.

LULU: He slept in today. How much d'you want?

SCHIGOLCH: Two hundred, if you've got it on you. Three hundred if you like. A couple of my regulars have done a bunk.

LULU: (*Goes to the writing-desk and fumbles in a drawer.*) God, I'm tired!

SCHIGOLCH: (*Looking round.*) Me too. That's what made me come over. I've been wanting to see how you were living for ages.

LULU: Well?

SCHIGOLCH: It's all too much. (*Looking around.*) This was me fifty years ago. Hell, you've done well for yourself. (*Scraping his foot.*) The carpets...

LULU: (*Giving him two notes.*) I like walking barefoot best.

SCHIGOLCH: (*Looking at her portrait.*) Is that you?

LULU: (*A twinkle in her eye.*) Not bad, eh. – Time for a quick one?

SCHIGOLCH: What you got?

LULU: (*Getting up.*) Spa Elixir.

SCHIGOLCH: It won't do me much good. – Does he drink?

LULU: (*Takes a carafe and glasses from a cupboard by the fireplace.*) Not yet. (*Coming downstage.*) Comfort takes people different ways.

SCHIGOLCH: He gets violent?

LULU: (*Filling two glasses.*) Falls asleep.

SCHIGOLCH: When he's drunk you can see what makes him tick.

LULU: I'd rather not. (*Sits opposite SCHIGOLCH.*) So tell me.

SCHIGOLCH: The streets get longer and longer, and my legs get shorter.

LULU: And your concertina?

SCHIGOLCH: Sprung a leak, like me and my asthma. Only I keep thinking, what's the point of getting it put right?

32

(*Clinks her glass.*)

LULU: (*Empties hers.*) I thought you'd had your lot.

SCHIGOLCH: So did I. But as soon as the sun goes down, I find I can't sit still. I'm looking forward to winter. I expect by then my (*He coughs.*) asthma will have found me a get-out clause.

LULU: D'you think they might've forgotten about you on the other side?

SCHIGOLCH: Could be. It don't go alphabetical, you know. (*Stroking her knee.*) Now you tell me...it's been a long time...my little Lulu.

LULU: (*Pulls back, smiling.*) Life beats me sometimes.

SCHIGOLCH: What do you know? You're still so young.

LULU: You calling me Lulu.

SCHIGOLCH: In't it Lulu? I never called you anything else...?

LULU: I've not been Lulu since the Flood.

SCHIGOLCH: Well the principle's the same.

LULU: You reckon?

SCHIGOLCH: What's it now?

LULU: Eve.

SCHIGOLCH: What'd I tell you!

LULU: It's what I answer to anyway.

SCHIGOLCH: (*Looking round.*) This is what I dreamed of for you. You were destined for this. Who'd have envisaged royal luxury like this!

LULU: When I think back – huh!

SCHIGOLCH: (*Stroking her knee.*) So how are things? Still taking French?

LULU: I lie around and sleep.

SCHIGOLCH: Very good. That always makes a good impression. – What else?

LULU: What's it to you?

SCHIGOLCH: What's it to me! I'd sooner live till Judgement Day and forego all the pleasures of heaven than leave my Lulu in need down here. I may have made my peace with my better self, but I still know what makes the world go round.

LULU: I don't.

SCHIGOLCH: You're too well off.

LULU: (*Shudders.*) Like hell...

SCHIGOLCH: Better'n with your old dancing bear? He's passed on too now.

LULU: I'm just...

(*Stops herself.*)

SCHIGOLCH: Say what's on your mind, littl'un. I had faith in you when all there was to see were those two great big eyes. – You're just what?

LULU: An animal.

SCHIGOLCH: And what an animal! A thoroughbred! I can rest easy with that. We ain't got time for disapproval. What are we anyway but decay?

LULU: Thanks a lot. I like to think I'm reasonably appetising.

SCHIGOLCH: So we are.

LULU: Your guests would hardly overeat.

SCHIGOLCH: Just you wait!

(*Rises.*)

LULU: (*Rising.*) Is that enough?

SCHIGOLCH: I'll find my own way out.

(*He goes. LULU accompanies him and comes back with Dr SCHOEN.*)

SCHOEN: What's your father doing here, Madam?

LULU: What's the matter with you?

SCHOEN: If I were your husband, Madam, I wouldn't give the man houseroom.

LULU: (*Realising.*) Relax. He's not here. – I don't understand.

SCHOEN: I know. (*Offering her a chair.*) It's something I'd like to talk to you about.

LULU: (*Sitting nervously.*) Why didn't you say something yesterday?

SCHOEN: Please, we won't mention yesterday now.

LULU: (*Nervous.*) Oh I see. (*Clears her throat.*)

SCHOEN: I want you to stop calling on me.

LULU: Can I offer you –

SCHOEN: Thank you, no Elixir. D'you understand me?

(*LULU shakes her head.*) Very well. You have the choice.
Either you behave as befits your position –

LULU: Or?

SCHOEN: Or I shall be forced to turn to the person
responsible for the way you behave.

LULU: How d'you see yourself managing that?!

SCHOEN: I shall ask your husband to supervise your
movements himself. (*LULU gets up and goes to the stairs
left.*) Where are you going?

LULU: Walter!

SCHOEN: (*Jumps up.*) Are you mad?

LULU: (*Turning back.*) Aha! (*Comes down the stairs, puts
SCHOEN's arm round her neck.*) Why are you still afraid,
when you're so close to fulfilling your desire?

SCHOEN: Don't fool about. I'm engaged – at last. My only
desire is to admit my wife to a respectable home.

LULU: (*Sitting.*) We can meet wherever you think fit.

SCHOEN: We will meet nowhere, except in the presence of
your husband!

LULU: You don't even believe that yourself.

SCHOEN: Then he must be made to. Call him! Since his
marriage to you, because of all I've done for him, he's
become my friend.

LULU: (*Rising.*) Mine too. You get a whole load of friends,
the moment you marry a pretty young wife.

SCHOEN: You think all women are like you! That man is
still a child at heart. Or he'd have been on to your
peccadillos ages ago.

LULU: He's not a child, he's just boring. He sees nothing.
Not me, not himself. He's blind, blind, blind...! (*Pause.*)
I'm mouldering away! Neglecting myself. He calls me
his treasure, his little rascal. Talks to me like some...
piano tutor! (*Pause.*) He makes no claims on me.
Everything's fine by him. And the reason? He's never in
his life felt the need for a woman.

SCHOEN: You really think so?

LULU: He admits it quite freely. He's afraid of women.
He's nervous about his health.

SCHOEN: How many women would count themselves blessed in your position?

LULU: (*Pleading tenderly.*) Lead him astray. Get him into bad company. You know the right people. All I am to him is a wife. I feel so ridiculous. I rack my brains, night and day, for a way to shake him out of it. I'm so desperate, I dance can-can. He yawns and mutters about obscenity.

SCHOEN: Nonsense, he's an artist.

LULU: Only when I model for him. He also thinks he's famous.

SCHOEN: It's we who've made him so.

LULU: But he believes everything! When we first met, I let him think I'd never made love... (*SCHOEN falls into an armchair.*) Otherwise he'd have looked on me as a fallen woman. I've even started dreaming about Goll.

SCHOEN: At least he wasn't boring.

LULU: It's like he never went away. He isn't angry with me, just terribly, terribly sad. The only thing is, he can't get over how much money I've frittered away since then.

SCHOEN: You're missing the rod.

LULU: Perhaps. I've stopped dancing.

SCHOEN: Educate him to it.

LULU: It's a waste of time.

SCHOEN: Out of every hundred women you'll find ninety educating their husbands.

LULU: He loves me.

SCHOEN: Yes well, that is fatal.

LULU: He doesn't know me, but he loves me! If he had just a half-way decent understanding of me, he'd tie a rock round my neck and drop me in the deepest part of the ocean!

SCHOEN: (*Rising.*) Are we finished now?

LULU: Feel free.

SCHOEN: Twice I've married you off. I've given your husband status. You live in luxury. If that's not enough for you, leave me out of it!

LULU: (*Determined.*) If I belong to anyone on this earth, I belong to you. Without you I'd be... I won't say where. You took me by the hand, fed and clothed me when I'd tried to steal your watch. D'you think I can forget that? Anyone else would've called the police. You sent me to school, had me learn manners – who else in the whole world would've given me the time of day? I've danced and sat as a model and been happy I was able to earn a living at it. But loving to order, I can't do it.

SCHOEN: (*Raising his voice.*) Leave me our of it. My involvement has cost me enough already. I'd imagined that with a healthy young man a woman of your age couldn't ask for more. You'd finally be content. If you feel you owe me anything, don't throw yourself at me a third time. Am I to wait even longer to turn my pickings into solid benefit? What good to me is your being married, if people see you coming in and out of my house every hour of the day? Why, oh why couldn't Doktor Goll have lasted another year? He kept you under lock and key. And I'd have my wife home and dry!

LULU: And then where would you be? That girl will get on your nerves. She's been brought up too well. What do I care if you get married? But you're fooling yourself if you think you can unload your self-disgust on me!

SCHWARZ: (*Brush in hand, appearing in the doorway, left.*) What's going on?

LULU: (*To SCHOEN.*) Go on, tell him.

SCHWARZ: What's the matter?

LULU: None of your business.

SCHOEN: Shut up!

LULU: I'm becoming too much.

(*SCHWARZ takes LULU off left. SCHOEN flicks through the pages of a book on the table.*)

SCHWARZ: (*Returning.*) Is this some kind of joke?

SCHOEN: (*Indicating a chair.*) Please.

SCHWARZ: What's wrong?

SCHOEN: Please.

SCHWARZ: (*Sitting.*) Well?

SCHOEN: (*Sitting.*) You married half a million.

SCHWARZ: Is that a crime?

SCHOEN: You've made a name for yourself. You need deny yourself nothing –

SCHWARZ: Do you two know something I don't?

SCHOEN: For six months you've had your head in the clouds. You have a wife whose qualities would be the envy of any man, and who deserves a man she can respect –

SCHWARZ: You mean she doesn't?

SCHOEN: No.

SCHWARZ: (*Taken aback.*)…I come from a poor background. She's more upper class. My dearest wish is to become her equal in breeding. (*Offering SCHOEN his hand.*) I thank you.

SCHOEN: (*Embarrassed, holding his hand.*) Please…please…

SCHWARZ: (*Steeling himself.*) Tell me!

SCHOEN: Keep more of an eye on her.

SCHWARZ: Me? Her!

SCHOEN: We're not children any more. This isn't a game. She needs to be taken seriously.

SCHWARZ: What's she doing then?

SCHOEN: First, count up all the things you have to thank her for –

SCHWARZ: What's she doing – for God's sake!

SCHOEN: Then hold yourself responsible for your mistakes, and no one else.

SCHWARZ: Who with? Who with?

SCHOEN: If we were to fight a duel…

SCHWARZ: For how long?

SCHOEN: (*Evasive.*) I haven't come here to cause a scandal. I've come to save you from scandal.

SCHWARZ: (*Shaking his head.*) You've got her all wrong.

SCHOEN: (*Embarrassed.*) I cannot continue to see you live in ignorance. The girl deserves a decent family life. Ever since I've known her, she's always changed for the better.

SCHWARZ: Ever since…when? How long have you known her then?

SCHOEN: Roughly from her twelfth year.

SCHWARZ: (*Confused.*) She's never told me this.

SCHOEN: She used to sell flowers outside the Alhambra Café. She'd push her way barefoot through the customers every night from twelve till two. I'm telling you this so you realise this is not a question of moral depravity.

SCHWARZ: She said she grew up with an aunt.

SCHOEN: That was the woman I entrusted her to.

SCHWARZ: (*Sobs.*) Oh God!

SCHOEN: (*Firmly.*) No 'Oh Gods', please. I'm speaking frankly and offering my assistance. Don't show yourself unworthy.

SCHWARZ: (*From here on breaks up more and more.*) When I met her she told me she'd never loved.

SCHOEN: That, from a widow?

SCHWARZ: He made her wear short skirts! – How did he come to know her then?

SCHOEN: Through me. After the death of my wife, when I was first approaching my present fiancée. She tried to stand in my way. She'd got it in her head to marry me.

SCHWARZ: (*Struck by the awful realisation.*) And then when her husband died?

SCHOEN: You married half a million!

SCHWARZ: (*Wailing.*) If only I'd stayed as I was. Died of hunger!

SCHOEN: (*Superior.*) People make allowances. You're an artist. – With that father of hers, it's a miracle she's turned out as well as she has.

SCHWARZ: But he died in an asylum.

SCHOEN: He was here just now!

SCHWARZ: Here? In my house?

SCHOEN: He was sneaking away as I got here. You can see, the glasses are still here.

SCHWARZ: She said he died in an asylum.

SCHOEN: (*The pep talk.*) Let her know who's boss! She asks no more than to be allowed to show total obedience. Being with Doktor Goll was like paradise for her. And he was not a man to be trifled with.

SCHWARZ: (*Shaking his head.*) She said she'd never loved...

SCHOEN: Pull yourself together.

SCHWARZ: She swore!

SCHOEN: You can't demand a sense of duty without recognising your own.

SCHWARZ: On her mother's grave!

SCHOEN: She never knew her mother. Let alone the grave. – This is a decisive moment. You could lose her tomorrow.

SCHWARZ: If only I could cry! If only I could scream! (*Gets up, apparently calm.*) You're right, quite right.

SCHOEN: (*Grabbing his hand.*) Where are you going?

SCHWARZ: To talk to her.

SCHOEN: Quite right. (*Accompanies him to the right-hand door, then comes back.*) That was a job and a half. (*A pause, then he looks to the left.*) But he took her into the studio. (*A terrible groan off right. He rushes to the door right, finds it locked.*) Open up! Open up!

LULU: (*Emerging from the left doorway.*) What's going on?

SCHOEN: Open up!

LULU: (*Coming down the stairs.*) This is awful.

SCHOEN: D'you have a meat-cleaver or something, in the kitchen?

LULU: He'll open up…when he's finished crying.

SCHOEN: (*Kicking the door.*) Open up!

LULU: Shouldn't we send for a doctor?

SCHOEN: Are you out of your mind?

LULU: This serves you right.

(*A bell sounds in the hall. SCHOEN and LULU stare at each other.*)

SCHOEN: (*Creeps upstage, stops in the doorway.*) I can't be seen here now.

LULU: It could be his dealer.

(*The bell rings again.*)

SCHOEN: But if we don't answer… (*LULU creeps towards the door.*) Stop. (*He goes out on tiptoe. LULU returns to the locked door and listens. SCHOEN comes back with ALVA.*) Please keep calm.

ALVA: (*Very excited.*) Revolution's broken out in Paris.

SCHOEN: Be quiet.

ALVA: (*To LULU.*) You're white as a sheet.

SCHOEN: (*Rattling the door-handle.*) Walter! Walter!
(*We hear his death rattle.*)

LULU: May God forgive you –

SCHOEN: Did you bring the cleaver?

LULU: If we've got one…
(*Goes off, hesitantly, right.*)

SCHOEN: Revolution in Paris?

ALVA: They're running round in circles back at the office.
No one knows what to write.

SCHOEN: (*Kicking the door.*) Walter! (*The bell rings in the
hall.*) Who else is going to turn up! (*Straightening up.*)
Has his fun in life and leaves others to pick up the
pieces!

LULU: (*Returning with the cleaver.*) Henrietta's come back.

SCHOEN: Then shut the door after you.

ALVA: Give it here.
(*Takes the cleaver and jams it between the door-post and the
lock.*)

SCHOEN: Hold it firmer.

ALVA: It's coming.
(*The door jumps out of its lock. He drops the cleaver and
tumbles back. Pause.*)

LULU: (*To SCHOEN, pointing to the door.*) After you.
(*SCHOEN shies away.*) Feeling faint? (*SCHOEN wipes
sweat from his brow and enters. LULU holds on to the door-
post, raises her fingers to her mouth and screams suddenly.*)
Oh! (*Rushes over to ALVA.*) I can't stay here.

ALVA: To cut your own throat…

LULU: (*Taking his hand.*) Come with me.

ALVA: Where?

LULU: I can't be alone.

SCHOEN: (*Comes back, a set of keys in his hand which is
covered in blood, and shuts the door behind him.*) Tell
Henrietta to fetch Doktor Bernstein. And then the police.
(*LULU goes.*) Where was she going?

ALVA: To her room. To change.
(*Pause.*)

SCHOEN: This is a judgement.

ALVA: It made my blood freeze.

SCHOEN: The fool!

ALVA: The penny finally dropped, did it?

SCHOEN: He was too wrapped up in himself. (*Pause. LULU comes back in hat and coat.*) Where's he keep his papers?

LULU: In the writing-desk.

SCHOEN: (*At the desk.*) Whereabouts?

LULU: Bottom right. (*Kneels in front of the writing-desk, opens a drawer and tips the paper on the floor.*) There. There's nothing to be afraid of. He had no secrets.

SCHOEN: I might as well retire right now. (*Pointing right.*) There goes my engagement!

ALVA: If you play with fire –

SCHOEN: Why don't you shout it out in the street!

ALVA: (*Indicates LULU.*) If you'd done the decent thing by her when her mother died –

LULU: (*Getting up.*) I'm not staying here a moment longer.

SCHOEN: The late edition will be out in an hour. I can't be seen on the streets.

ALVA: You'll have to go away.

SCHOEN: And leave the field to the scandal-mongers?

LULU: (*By the chaise-longue.*) Ten minutes ago he was lying here.

SCHOEN: That's the thanks I get for all I did for him. Within a few moments he dashes my life to pieces!

ALVA: Control yourself, please!

LULU: (*On the chaise-longue.*) Why? We're among friends.

SCHOEN: What will you tell the police?

LULU: Nothing. He was always talking about death.

ALVA: And yet he had everything we didn't.

SCHOEN: (*Flaring up suddenly.*) Why should I listen to you! If you do everything in your power to avoid having brothers and sisters, all the more reason for me to bring up other children!

ALVA: You don't know people at all, do you.

LULU: You could always put out your own late edition.

ALVA: Our editors are stunned. Everything's ground to a halt.

SCHOEN: Maybe that's a way out... We could say he had a persecution complex. If only the police would come! Time is precious.

(*A bell sounds in the corridor.*)

ALVA: They're here.

(*SCHOEN turns to the door.*)

LULU: Wait. You've got blood...I'll wipe it off. (*Does.*)

SCHOEN: Your husband's.

LULU: It won't stain.

SCHOEN: You monster!

LULU: You know, you'll marry me in the end.

Scene 3

Theatre dressing-room, lined in red fabric. The door upstage left. Upstage right a screen. In the centre, end on towards the audience, a long table, on which dance costumes are laid. An armchair each side of the table. Down left a small table with an armchair. Down right a tall mirror, and next to it a very wide, high, old-fashioned armchair. A powder-puff, make-up box etc. in front of the mirror.

ALVA: (*Down left, fills two glasses with champagne and red wine.*) In all my years in the theatre, I've never seen an audience so beside themselves.

LULU: (*Invisible, behind the screen.*) Don't give me too much wine. – Is he watching tonight?

ALVA: Father? I don't even know if he's in.

LULU: I'm sure he doesn't want to see me.

ALVA: He has so little time.

LULU: Too busy with his fiancée.

ALVA: No, playing the market. He never lets up. (*As SCHOEN enters.*) We were just talking about you.

LULU: Is that him?

SCHOEN: You're changing?

LULU: (*Looking over the top of the screen.*) You say in all the papers I'm the most inspiring dancer ever to tread the boards, but you don't even find me inspiring enough to find out for yourself.

SCHOEN: I've been too busy writing. – You should come downstage a bit more.

ALVA: She was sticking strictly to her role.

SCHOEN: Then you ought to make more use of your performers. (*To LULU.*) What d'you come on as next?

LULU: A flower-girl.

SCHOEN: In tights?

ALVA: No, ankle-length skirt.

SCHOEN: A vision like her really doesn't need all this symbolic nonsense of yours. It's what the audience wants that matters.

ALVA: They hardly seem to be bored.

SCHOEN: Of course not. Because I've been working on the press for the past six months. – Has the Prince been by?

ALVA: No one's been by. – Who's this prince? Not Escerny?

SCHOEN: Shall I see you later? At Peter's?

ALVA: At midnight?

SCHOEN: Midnight. (*Goes.*)

LULU: I'd given up hope of his coming.

ALVA: Don't let that grumpy fault-finding of his put you off. Just be careful not to wear yourself out before the last number.

LULU: (*Comes out from behind the screen in an antique-style, ankle-length, armless, white dress with a red border, a colourful crown in her hair, and a basket of flowers in her hand.*) He just doesn't realise how cleverly you use your performers.

ALVA: I knew you'd understand the art of costume changing.

LULU: If I'd tried selling flowers outside the Alhambra like this, they'd have locked me up straight off.

ALVA: Why! You were just a child.

LULU: D'you remember the first time I came to your room?

ALVA: (*Nods.*) You wore a dark-blue dress with black velvet.

LULU: I had to hide and we didn't know where.

ALVA: My mother had been bed-ridden two years.

LULU: You were playing with your toy theatre and asked me to join you. I can still see you, moving the little figures back and forward.

ALVA: For years it remained my most awful memory – suddenly realising what was really going on.

LULU: You became very cool towards me.

ALVA: I revered you perhaps more than my mother. D'you remember when she died? I was seventeen. I went straight to my father and insisted he made you his wife forthwith – or we'd have to fight a duel.

LULU: He told me.

ALVA: Now he's dreaming up some plot to have me work against his marriage to the Countess.

LULU: Does she still have such an innocent view of the world?

ALVA: She loves him. I think she'd sacrifice anything for him.

LULU: (*Holding out her glass.*) Just another drop, please.

ALVA: (*Pouring.*) You're drinking too much.

LULU: He's got to learn to believe in my success! All he believes in is newspapers.

ALVA: He believes in nothing.

LULU: He brought me into the theatre so someone rich enough to marry me would eventually discover me. I'm supposed to look forward to dancing my way into some millionaire's heart!

ALVA: Heaven forbid you're taken away from us. You know I've always wanted to write a play for you.

LULU: But I'm not cut out for the stage.

ALVA: You were born a dancer.

LULU: Why don't you make your plays as interesting as life?

ALVA: Because no one would believe us.

LULU: In real life all this mumbo-jumbo wouldn't make a cat look twice. You know, one or two people out there go into quite a serious huddle with themselves over what we do.

ALVA: How can you tell?

LULU: I get this huge chill up my spine.

ALVA: You're incredible…

(*An electric bell rings above the door.*)

45

LULU: My shawl.

ALVA: (*Spreads a wide shawl around her shoulders.*) Here.

LULU: I shall try to live up to his shameless publicity.
(*LULU goes. ALVA sits, left, takes out a notebook and makes a note. He looks up.*)

ALVA: Act One: Doktor Goll. What's the point? Even if I had him talking direct from hell, or wherever he's paying for his orgies, they'd make me pay for his sins. (*The strongly muffled sound of lengthy applause and shouts of 'Bravo' are heard off.*) It's like the zoo at feeding time out there. – Act Two: Walter Schwarz – even less likely. How people reveal themselves when misfortune strikes! Act Three? Prince Escerny? It can't go on this way. (*The electric bell above the door rings out and continues ringing. ALVA jumps up.*) My God, what's happening? Something's wrong. All hell must've broken loose.
(*He goes. Pause. LULU comes in, crosses the stage and sits in the armchair by the mirror. ALVA follows almost immediately.*)

ALVA: You fainted?

LULU: Did you see him?

ALVA: Who?

LULU: With his fiancée?

ALVA: With his – (*To SCHOEN, who enters.*) You could've spared her that!

SCHOEN: What's the matter with her? (*To LULU.*) How dare you play that scene at me!

LULU: I feel like I've been lashed.

SCHOEN: (*Locking the door.*) You'll go back on. Don't forget I'm carrying the responsibility for all this.

LULU: Who to? Your bride?

SCHOEN: What difference does that make? You're employed here, you earn a wage…you dance for anyone who buys a ticket.

ALVA: (*To LULU.*) Please, tell me what to do. (*A knock on the door.*) All right, all right, just a minute. (*To LULU.*) You don't want us to cancel the performance, do you?

LULU: Just give me a moment. Right now I can't do a thing. Bring the next number forward. No one'll notice whether I dance now or in five minutes' time. My legs just won't carry me.

ALVA: But then you'll dance?

LULU: As best as I can.

ALVA: (*In response to continued knocking.*) I'm coming. (*Off.*)

LULU: You're right to put me in my place. And you couldn't have done it better than show me doing the skirt-dance to your fiancée.

SCHOEN: Given your background, you're lucky even to be appearing in front of respectable people.

LULU: Even when, faced with my vulgarity, you don't know which way to turn.

SCHOEN: Rubbish! Your vulgarity is what you're paid for – every step. One shouts 'Bravo', the other boos – to you it's all the same. Can you imagine a more magnificent triumph than a respectable girl hardly able to stay in her seat?

LULU: I don't give a damn what people think. The last thing I want is to be better than I really am. This way I feel easy.

SCHOEN: (*Moral outrage.*) Now you're showing your true colours!

LULU: I never imagined I'd achieve even the slightest self-respect.

SCHOEN: (*Suddenly suspecting.*) Don't pretend to feel sorry for yourself.

LULU: I know only too well what would've become of me if you hadn't saved me from it.

SCHOEN: D'you really think you're any different now?

LULU: No, thank God. (*Laughs.*) And it makes me happier than I can say!

SCHOEN: So will you dance now?

LULU: Yes. I don't care where or what.

SCHOEN: Then get on stage!

LULU: (*Begging like a child.*) Just a bit longer. Please. I can't even stand. They'll ring.

SCHOEN: This is what you've come to – in spite of all the sacrifices I've made for your welfare and upbringing.

LULU: (*Ironic.*) You mean you overestimated your
   ennobling influence?

SCHOEN: Spare me your sarcasm.

LULU: The Prince was here. He's taking me to Africa.

SCHOEN: To Africa?

LULU: Why not? You turned me into a dancer so someone
   would come along and take me off.

SCHOEN: But not to Africa!

LULU: Then why didn't you just let me faint and quietly
   thank your lucky stars?

SCHOEN: Because, sad to say, I didn't believe your
   fainting was real.

LULU: (*Mocking.*) You mean you couldn't stand it out there?
   You were afraid I might really have hurt myself?

SCHOEN: I know only too well you're indestructable. –
   Stop looking at me like that!

LULU: No one's keeping you here.

SCHOEN: I'll go, as soon as the bell rings.

LULU: As soon as you've got your strength back. – Where
   is all your strength, by the way? You've been engaged
   three years. Why don't you get married? You know of no
   obstacle. Why blame it on me? You ordered me to marry
   Doktor Goll. You make artists your creatures, princes
   your proteges. Why don't you marry yourself?

SCHOEN: (*Furious.*) I suppose you think you're standing in
   my way!

LULU: (*From now till the end in triumph.*) If only you knew
   how happy your anger makes me. You do everything a
   man can to humiliate a woman. Because that way you
   hope you can put me behind you. But your self-control's
   running out. I can tell. Go then! For the sake of your
   innocent bride, leave me in peace! A minute longer and
   your mood will change, and you'll be making a scene
   you can't answer for now.

SCHOEN: I'm not afraid of you any more.

LULU: It's yourself you need to be afraid of! You know I
   don't need to faint to destroy your future. It's not just as
   some femme fatale you see me. You also think I'm the

salt of the earth. In fact I'm neither one nor the other. The sad thing for you is that's how you see me.

SCHOEN: (*Desperate.*) Never mind what I think. Take the Prince, dance him into the ground! In a week I'll be married. And I beg you – by the good I know is in you – not to let me set eyes on you again!

LULU: I'll lock all my doors.

SCHOEN: That's right, show off! As God is my witness, I have never in all my days cursed anyone as much as you.

LULU: And all because of my poor background.

SCHOEN: Because of your depravity!

LULU: I'm only too happy to take the blame. You need to feel pure, or you can't marry the poor, innocent child.

SCHOEN: You're asking to feel the weight of my hand!

LULU: (*Quick.*) Yes! Yes! What do I have to say to make you do it? I wouldn't swop with that girl for all the world. And yet she loves you as no woman has ever loved you!

SCHOEN: Silence, woman, silence!

LULU: Marry her. Then I can watch her dance in her artless misery instead of having her watch me.

SCHOEN: (*Raising his fist.*) God forgive me...

LULU: Hit me, go on! Where've you put your riding whip? Slap my legs.

SCHOEN: (*Clutches his temples.*) Away, away! (*Rushes to the door, thinks a moment, then turns.*) I can't go to her like this...I'll go home... If I could look the world in the face.

LULU: Be a man, can't you? Just look at your face. Not a trace of conscience. You're quite prepared, in cold blood, to make the girl who loves you unhappy. You conquer half the world, you do exactly as you please, and yet you know as well as I –

SCHOEN: (*Collapses exhausted in a chair left of the centre table.*) Shut up!

LULU: – you're too weak to tear yourself away from me.

SCHOEN: (*Groaning.*) The poor, innocent child!

LULU: He weeps like a child, the awesome potentate! How come the devil incarnate suddenly becomes so weak? – You may go now. You mean nothing to me any more.

SCHOEN: I can't go to her.

LULU: Get out of here! Come back when you've got your strength back.

SCHOEN: For God's sake, tell me what I should do.

LULU: (*Rises, her coat stays on the chair. Pushing the costumes on the middle table aside.*) Here's some notepaper...

SCHOEN: I can't write...

LULU: (*Standing behind him, propped on the arm of his chair.*) Write! 'My dear Countess...'

SCHOEN: I call her Adelheid.

LULU: 'My dear Countess... Release me from your promise. I cannot in all conscience...' (*As SCHOEN puts the pen down and looks up at her, pleading.*) ...write 'conscience...join your fate with mine.'

SCHOEN: (*Writing.*) You're right, you're quite right...

LULU: 'I give you my word that I am unworthy of your love.' (*As SCHOEN turns away once again.*) ...write it: 'love... These lines are the proof. For three years I've been trying to tear myself free. But I don't have the strength. I am writing to you at the side of the woman who holds me in her power. Forget me. Doktor Ludwig Schoen.'

SCHOEN: (*Groaning.*) Oh God!

LULU: (*Half shocked.*) No 'Oh Gods' please. (*Emphatic.*) 'PS. Do not try to save me.'

(*SCHOEN writes.*)

Scene 4

A sumptuous drawing-room in German Renaissance style with a heavy carved oak ceiling. Dark wooden relief halfway up the walls. Above them, on either side, faded tapestries. Above, at the back the room ends in a curtained gallery, from which a monumental staircase left leads down halfway across the stage. In the centre, beneath the gallery, the main door, with spiral pillars and pediment. A large, high fireplace against the right wall. Further downstage a French window behind heavy, closed curtains. By the foot of the staircase left, a closed doorway in Genoan velvet.

In front of the fireplace, a Chinese folding screen. LULU's portrait as a pierrot in an antique-style gold frame stands on a decorative easel in front of a pillar at the foot of the staircase bannister. Down left a wide ottoman, down right of that an armchair. In the middle of the room a heavy, four-sided table, around which are three high-backed, upholstered chairs. A white bouquet in the middle of the table.

GESCHWITZ: (*On the ottoman, in a fur-trimmed Hussar-bodice with a tall, stand-up collar, gigantic cuff-buttons, a veil over her face, her hands forced into a muff, to LULU.*) I can't tell you how much I'm looking forward to seeing you at our lady artists' ball.

SCHOEN: (*Down left.*) Is there no way we men can smuggle ourselves in?

GESCHWITZ: It would be high treason for any of us to even countenance such a plan.

SCHOEN: (*Crosses to the centre table.*) Magnificent flowers.

LULU: (*In the armchair, wearing a day-dress with large flowers, her hair in a simple bun with a golden clasp.*) Fraulein von Geschwitz brought them for me.

GESCHWITZ: It was nothing. – You won't forget to dress as a man, will you?

LULU: D'you think I'll look right?

GESCHWITZ: (*Indicating the picture.*) You look a dream in this.

LULU: My husband doesn't like it.

GESCHWITZ: Is it by someone I know?

LULU: You wouldn't have met him.

GESCHWITZ: He's no longer alive?

SCHOEN: (*Down right, his voice deep.*) He couldn't take it any more.

LULU: Something wrong?
(*SCHOEN controls himself.*)

GESCHWITZ: (*Rising.*) I can't stay any longer. We have a life-class tonight, and I've still so much to get ready for the ball. – Herr Doktor.
(*Accompanied by LULU, she goes off through the centre door.*)

SCHOEN: (*Looking around.*) This place is a disgrace! The twilight of my days – ha! Show me one corner that hasn't been defiled. Thirty years' work, and this is my hearth and home! (*Looking around.*) God knows who's listening to me now. (*Pulls a revolver from his breast pocket.*) You walk in fear of your life. (*With the revolver cocked, he goes to the curtains right, lifts them and finds no one hidden behind them.*) Filth everywhere. Filth...
(*Shakes his head and crosses left then hides the revolver as he hears LULU coming.*)

LULU: Couldn't you take time off this afternoon?

SCHOEN: What did the Countess really want?

LULU: She wants to paint me. – Couldn't you take time off? I'd so love to drive through the gardens with you.

SCHOEN: The very day I have to be at the Exchange. You know I'm not free this afternoon. My entire fortune is at stake.

LULU: I'd sooner be six foot under than let my entire life be so soured by my possessions.

SCHOEN: Once you take life easy, death comes even easier.

LULU: (*Around his neck.*) You worry too much. I've hardly seen you for weeks. Months.

SCHOEN: (*Stroking her hair.*) Your sense of fun was supposed to cheer the winter of my life.

LULU: But you didn't marry me.

SCHOEN: I didn't marry anyone else.

LULU: I married you!

SCHOEN: What difference does that make?

LULU: I was always afraid it would change everything.

SCHOEN: It's trampled on a great many things.

LULU: But not one.

SCHOEN: What's that?

LULU: You still love me.
(*SCHOEN's face twitches. He indicates she should go first. They go off left. Countess GESCHWITZ opens the central door cautiously, steps forward and listens, then shrinks back as voices are heard on the gallery.*)

GESCHWITZ: Oh God, someone's coming.

(*Hides behind the screen.*)

SCHIGOLCH: (*Coming down the stairs, followed by RODRIGO.*) Oh it's good to be home again! What bastard's waxed the stairs? They're a bloody obstacle course. – Come on, don't he shy! We'll start with a drop of something money can't buy. (*Opens a small cupboard under the stairs, puts two bottles and two glasses on the table.*) I started one of 'em yesterday. (*He fills the glasses, then leans on the table, propping himself up.*) Would sir care for a smoke? I've got everything. You just have to ask. (*Sits.*)

RODRIGO: Who lives here anyway?

SCHIGOLCH: We do! Regular as clockwork. Every Stock Exchange day. Cheers!

(*They clink glasses.*)

RODRIGO: Here's to Doctor Death!

SCHIGOLCH: And Jumping Jack! If something better turns up, I can up sticks any time, but then again...

LULU: (*Entering left in an elegant Parisian ball-gown, with a wide décolleté trimmed with flowers, and more in her hair.*) Boys, boys, I'm expecting visitors.

SCHIGOLCH: Then I'd better have a button-hole too.

(*Fumbles in the bouquet.*)

LULU: Do I look all right?

SCHIGOLCH: What's this you've got up front?

LULU: Orchids. (*Leans forward.*) Smell.

RODRIGO: You must be expecting Prince Escerny?

LULU: Heaven forbid.

RODRIGO: So there's yet another one!

LULU: The Prince is off on a trip.

(*Hurries up the stairs to the gallery.*)

RODRIGO: (*To SCHIGOLCH.*) You know, he wanted to marry her originally.

SCHIGOLCH: (*Sticking a lily in his coat.*) I wanted to marry her originally. Who hasn't wanted to marry her originally! But no one regrets not marrying her in the end.

RODRIGO: You mean, she isn't your daughter?

SCHIGOLCH: She wouldn't dream of it.

RODRIGO: Who is her father then?

SCHIGOLCH: She never had one.

LULU: (*Coming down from the gallery.*) What did I never have?

RODRIGO/SCHIGOLCH: (*Together.*) A father.

LULU: That's right. I'm a miracle of nature.

SCHIGOLCH: Did you lock up up there?

LULU: Here's the key.

SCHIGOLCH: You should've left it in the lock.

LULU: Why!

SCHIGOLCH: So it can't be opened from outside.

RODRIGO: I thought he was at the Stock Exchange?

LULU: He is. But he's paranoid.

RODRIGO: I'll just grab him by the feet and – splat – he'll be sticking to the ceiling. Just look at that bicep.

LULU: Let's see.

RODRIGO: (*Thumping his arm.*) Granite. Cast iron.

LULU: (*Comparing RODRIGO's arm and her own.*) If only your ears weren't so long…

FERDINAND: (*Entering through the centre door.*) Doktor Schoen, Madam. (*Goes.*)

RODRIGO: (*Jumping up.*) The bastard! (*Goes behind the fire-screen.*) Saints preserve us!
(*Hides under the table.*)

SCHIGOLCH: Give me the key!
(*Takes it from LULU and drags himself up the stairs to the gallery.*)

ALVA: (*Enters in evening dress.*) I think we'll have to do the matinée by torchlight. I've – (*Notices SCHIGOLCH dragging himself painfully up the stairs.*) Who on earth's that?

LULU: An old friend of your father's.

ALVA: I've never seen him before.

LULU: They were in the army together.

ALVA: Is my father here then?

LULU: They had a drink together, but then he had to leave for the Exchange. (*FERDINAND comes back with a tray of food.*) But you'll have some lunch before we go? (*As ALVA keeps watching SCHIGOLCH.*) What do you think of me?

(*SCHIGOLCH finally leaves via the gallery.*)

ALVA: Shouldn't I keep that to myself?

LULU: I only meant my toilette.

ALVA: Your seamstress obviously knows you better than I…may allow myself to.

LULU: When I saw myself in the mirror, I almost wished I was a man – *my man!*
(*They sit at the table. FERDINAND serves cold snacks and champagne.*)

ALVA: (*To FERDINAND.*) Have you got toothache?

LULU: Don't.

FERDINAND: I'm sorry, Herr Doktor?

ALVA: You look a bit sorry for yourself.

FERDINAND: (*Through his teeth.*) I'm only human. (*Goes.*)

LULU: You know what I prize in you above all else? Your strength of character. You're so sure of yourself. Even when you've risked falling out with your father, you've always spoken up on my behalf.

ALVA: Let's not talk about it. It's just my fate…
(*Goes to lift the table-cloth.*)

LULU: (*Quickly.*) That was me.

ALVA: I don't believe it. – It's just fate that my most reckless ideas work out for the best.

LULU: You mustn't persuade yourself you're less good than you are.

ALVA: Why are you flattering me? No one could be worse than me – and have brought about so much good.

LULU: You're certainly the only man who's ever protected me without making me feel humiliated.

ALVA: D'you think it's been easy…?

SCHOEN: (*Appearing on the gallery between the middle pillars and carefully parting the curtains.*) My own son!

ALVA: …With gifts from heaven like yours, one turns those around one into criminals without realising… I'm only flesh and blood after all. If we hadn't grown up as brother and sister –

LULU: That's why I can be completely open only with you. From you I have nothing to fear.

ALVA: Believe me, there are moments when one feels one's
  entire being could disintegrate. The more self-control a
  man exercises, the more easily he breaks down.
  (*He goes to look under the table.*)
LULU: (*Quickly.*) What are you looking for?
ALVA: I beg you, let me believe what I want. You've meant
  more to me sacred and inviolable than you could to
  anyone else – for all your gifts.
LULU: How differently you think from your father.
  (*FERDINAND returns with more food and serves.*)
ALVA: (*To FERDINAND.*) Are you poorly or what?
LULU: Leave him alone.
ALVA: He's shaking like a leaf.
FERDINAND: I'm not used to waiting, that's all. Normally
  I'm just the coachman. (*Goes.*)
SCHOEN: So, him too...
  (*Takes position by the balustrade, hiding behind the curtain
  when necessary.*)
LULU: What moments did you mean, when your inner
  being could disintegrate?
ALVA: I didn't want to talk about this. Not over a glass of
  champagne.
LULU: I'm sorry if I've hurt you. I won't mention it again.
ALVA: Promise? For ever?
LULU: Shake on it. (*She offers her hand over the table. ALVA
  grasps it hesitantly, presses it to his own, then holds it
  passionately and at length to his lips.*) What are you doing?
  (*RODRIGO pokes his head out from the table. LULU looks
  daggers at him. RODRIGO goes back. SCHOEN sees him.*)
SCHOEN: And there's another one!
ALVA: (*Passionate.*) Mignon! Mignon!
LULU: (*Throws herself on the ottoman.*) Stop looking at me
  like that! For God's sake, let's go before it's too late.
  You're quite depraved!
ALVA: I told you I was the lowest of the low. I have no
  sense of honour, of pride...
LULU: And you think I'm the same?
ALVA: You? You stand so far above me...like...like the sun
  above an abyss. (*Kneels.*) Destroy me! I beg you, finish
  me off! Finish me off!

LULU: You mean, you love me?

ALVA: Do you love me? Mignon?

LULU: Me? – Not a soul. (*ALVA buries his head in her lap. LULU buries her hands in his hair.*) I poisoned your mother... (*RODRIGO sticks his head out, sees SCHOEN on the gallery and, through signs, draws his attention to LULU and ALVA. SCHOEN points his revolver at RODRIGO. RODRIGO ducks back under the table. LULU sees RODRIGO duck back, sees SCHOEN and jumps up. SCHOEN approaches them. ALVA remains motionless on his knees. SCHOEN takes him by the shoulder. ALVA rises, as if drunk with sleep. SCHOEN leads ALVA out through the centre door. RODRIGO makes a dash for the stairs. LULU stands in his way.*) Not this way.

RODRIGO: Let me by!

LULU: You'll run straight into him.

RODRIGO: He'll shoot my head off.

LULU: He's coming back.

RODRIGO: (*Tumbling back.*) Hell and damnation! (*Hides behind the curtains right.*)

SCHOEN: (*Comes back, locks the centre door, looks under the table.*) Where's he gone?

LULU: Out.

SCHOEN: How? Off the balcony?

LULU: He is an acrobat.

SCHOEN: How was I to know? (*Turning on LULU.*) You animal! You'll make a martyr of me yet with your gutter-tactics!

LULU: You should've brought me up better.

SCHOEN: You succubus! My fate is sealed! Drown in filth or become a murderer! You, the joy of my old age!

LULU: (*Cold-blooded.*) Just shut up and kill me.

SCHOEN: I've left you everything I own, and asked for nothing in return but the respect you'd expect from a visitor. Your credit is no longer good!

LULU: I'm good for a few years yet. (*Coming down the stairs.*) How d'you like my new dress?

SCHOEN: Out of my sight! I'm stuck with you like some incurable disease, and I want a cure. Do you understand

me? (*Presses the revolver on her.*) There's the prescription.
Administer it yourself.
(*LULU drops on the divan, her strength leaving her. She
turns the revolver this way and that.*)

LULU: It won't fire.

SCHOEN: D'you want me to show you how? (*As LULU
turns the revolver on him.*) Don't play games. (*LULU shoots
up at the ceiling. RODRIGO jumps out from behind the
curtains and runs up the stairs and off across the gallery.*)
What was that?

LULU: (*Innocent.*) Nothing.

SCHOEN: (*Lifting the curtains.*) Something flew out.

LULU: You're paranoid.

SCHOEN: How many more men have you got hidden
here? (*Snatches the revolver from her, flings back the curtains,
crosses and pulls back the fire-screen, grabs GESCHWITZ by
the collar and drags her downstage.*) Did you come down the
chimney, or what?

GESCHWITZ: (*Afraid for her life.*) Don't let him kill me!

SCHOEN: (*Shaking her.*) Or are you an acrobat too?

GESCHWITZ: (*A whimper.*) You're hurting me.

SCHOEN: (*Shaking her.*) You might as well stay for dinner
now. (*Drags her left, shoves her into the adjoining room and
locks the door after her.*) We don't want anyone making a
fuss. (*Sits next to LULU, forces the revolver on her.*) There
are still enough in there. – Look at me! Am I supposed
to indulge my coachman, when I daren't even put my
nose round the stable door?

LULU: Can you order up the carriage. Please. We're due at
the theatre.

SCHOEN: We're due in hell! (*Turning the revolver away from
himself and towards LULU's breast.*) D'you really think a
man can let himself be abused as you have abused me,
and still hesitate between a common scandal and the
benefit of freeing the world of you for ever? (*Holds her
down by the arm.*) Get on with it. It'll be the happiest
memory of my life. Fire away!

LULU: You can get a divorce.

SCHOEN: (*Rising.*) So someone else can pass the time of day where I've sunk from one degradation to the next? How can anyone divorce when they're so much a part of each other? It's like cutting off half of yourself. (*Reaching for the revolver.*) Give it here.

LULU: For pity's sake!

SCHOEN: I shall save you the trouble.

LULU: (*Tearing herself away from him, holding the revolver down, and in a self-possessed, decisive tone.*) People may have killed themselves for me, but that doesn't make me worthless. You knew why you married me. You may have sacrificed the 'evening of your days' on my account, but you've had my youth in return. I may not be sweet sixteen any more, but I'm still too young to die!

SCHOEN: (*Crowding in on her.*) Down, you murderer! Get down! On your knees! (*He forces her back to the staircase. Raising his hand.*) Down – and never dare to rise again! (*LULU sinks to her knees.*) Pray to God, murderess, that he gives you the strength!

RODRIGO: (*Re-appearing through the gallery curtains.*) Help! (*SCHOEN turns towards RODRIGO, turning his back on LULU. LULU fires five shots at SCHOEN and goes on pulling the trigger. SCHOEN pitches forwards and is caught by RODRIGO, who lowers him into a chair.*)

SCHOEN: And...yet...another one...

LULU: (*Rushing up to SCHOEN.*) My God!

SCHOEN: Out of my sight! Alva!

LULU: (*On her knees.*) The only man I ever loved.

SCHOEN: Whore! Assassin! – Alva! Alva! – Water!

LULU: Water. He needs water.
  (*Fills a glass with champagne.*)

ALVA: (*Enters from the gallery and down the stairs.*) Father! For God's sake! Father!

LULU: I shot him.

RODRIGO: She's innocent.

SCHOEN: (*To ALVA.*) You're here. – It didn't work.

ALVA: (*Goes to lift him.*) Let's get you to bed. Come on.

SCHOEN: No, don't move me. I'm parched. (*LULU approaches with the goblet of champagne.*) True to type.

(*Drinks, then turns to ALVA.*) Don't let her escape. You'll
be next.

ALVA: (*To RODRIGO.*) Help me get him to bed.

SCHOEN: No no. Please. No. Champagne, you murderess.

ALVA: (*To RODRIGO.*) Help me lift him. (*Points left.*) Into
the bedroom.

(*They lift SCHOEN and carry him right (sic.) LULU remains
by the table, the glass in her hand.*)

SCHOEN: (*Groaning.*) Oh God, oh God, oh God... (*ALVA
finds the door locked, turns the key and opens it. Countess
GESCHWITZ comes out. SCHOEN sees her and rises stiffly.*)
The devil – !

(*Crashes backwards on to the carpet.*)

LULU: (*Throws herself down by him, takes his head on her lap
and kisses him.*) He's found peace.

(*Rises, approaches the staircase.*)

ALVA: Stay right there!

GESCHWITZ: (*To LULU.*) I thought it was you.

LULU: (*Throwing herself at ALVA's feet.*) You mustn't turn me
in. I shot him because he would've shot me. I loved no
one in the world but him. Alva, ask anything you want.
Don't hand me over to the police! It would be such a
shame! I'm still young. I'll be true to you for the rest of
my life. I want to belong only to you. Look at me, Alva.
– For God's sake, look at me.

(*Knocking at the door, off.*)

ALVA: The police.

(*Goes to open the door.*)

End of Act One

ACT TWO
Pandora's Box

Scene 1

As in Scene Four, except that instead of the bouquet, a heavily veiled paraffin lamp stands on the centre table, spreading a muted light. ALVA is pacing up and down in front of the main door. RODRIGO, in servant's uniform, sits on the ottoman. Countess GESCHWITZ sits in the armchair left, dressed in a black, closely fitting dress, surrounded by cushions and with a rug over her knees. By her, on the table, is a coffee-machine and a cup of black coffee.

RODRIGO: He certainly knows how to keep us in suspense.

GESCHWITZ: Please. Could you just keep quiet?

RODRIGO: I don't see how all this can have changed her for the better.

GESCHWITZ: She looks more marvellous now than I've ever seen her.

RODRIGO: If this disease has hit her as bad as you, I'm broke. You've hardly got the strength to blow your nose.

GESCHWITZ: Anyone else would be six feet under. She draws health and strength from it.

RODRIGO: That's as may be. But I doubt if I'll be travelling with her tonight.

GESCHWITZ: You'd let your bride make the journey alone?

RODRIGO: The old man can protect her if it comes to it. Besides, I've got to wait here till my costumes are ready. I'll still get over the border in time. And meanwhile she'll have put on a bit of weight – hopefully. Then we'll get married, provided I can present her to a halfway decent audience. – That right, Herr Doktor?

ALVA: I'm afraid I wasn't listening.

RODRIGO: I wouldn't be involved in this at all if she hadn't kept tickling my fancy before the trial. I'd sooner take her to London and feed her up on plum duff for a couple of months.

GESCHWITZ: If only he'd get here!

RODRIGO: I've also got to get my props out of hock. I'd have been better off having the costumes made when we get there. A Parisian will decollete like there's no tomorrow. Whereas here they worry about bare skin like other countries worry about bombs. Two years ago at the Alhambra I got stung for a fifty mark fine because I showed a few hairs on my chest – less than you'd find on a toothbrush. I think the Minister of Culture decided schoolgirls could be put off knitting for life.

ALVA: The same curse hangs over our new writing: we're too literary. In my play 'Earth Spirit' I put all my effort into that principle. The woman, on whom the central character was based, has been behind bars a whole year. But because of that the play has only been produced on the liberal fringes of society. While my father was alive, every stage in Germany was open to my work. Things are very different now.

GESCHWITZ: The way the staff at the hospital avoided her yesterday was a sight to behold. A junior doctor bumped into me in the corridor and crumpled like he'd been hit by a bullet. The sisters hugged the walls. On the way back there wasn't a soul in sight. We couldn't have had a better opportunity – if only we'd had the damn passes. And now the wretch says he won't go with her!

ALVA: Fraulein Geschwitz, I still doubt whether your escape plan will work. But I can't tell you how impressed I've been by the sacrifice and superhuman contempt for death you've shown. I'm sure no man ever risked so much for a woman, let alone a friend. Your expenses in bringing all this about must have decimated your financial circumstances. Will you accept a loan of twenty thousand marks?

GESCHWITZ: We couldn't believe our luck when Sister Theophilia died! Without supervision we could swop beds as and when we wanted.

RODRIGO: I lay in that hospital a good three months, getting the lie of the land. What groom ever did more for his bride? My financial circumstances are also pretty decimated.

GESCHWITZ: He's coming!

(*Approaching footsteps get louder, then the curtain above the staircase parts and SCHIGOLCH steps out in a long, black, frock-coat and holding a white umbrella. Throughout the act his speech is interrupted by frequent yawning.*)

SCHIGOLCH: Damn dark in here. The sun's blinding outside.

GESCHWITZ: (*Painfully unwrapping her blanket.*) I'll be with you in a moment!

SCHIGOLCH: I've been touring round the junk shops since nine this morning. My legs are dangling like a couple of bell-clappers. This was supposed to be a new life from now on!

RODRIGO: Where are you hoping to stay tomorrow?

SCHIGOLCH: As long as it's not back in the 'Hotel Semolina' I don't mind.

RODRIGO: I can recommend an excellent hotel. I lived there with a lady lion-tamer. The people there were born in Berlin.

GESCHWITZ: (*Rising in her chair.*) Help me, can't you?

RODRIGO: (*Hurries over and supports her.*) You'll be safer from the police there than on the high wire!

GESCHWITZ: He's going to let you travel with her alone.

SCHIGOLCH: Don't tell me his chilblains are playing him up!

RODRIGO: I suppose you'd have me start my new engagement in dressing-gown and slippers?

ALVA: (*Holding a wallet, to GESCHWITZ, who stands propping herself up against the table.*) This contains ten thousand marks.

GESCHWITZ: Thank you, no.

ALVA: Please take it.

GESCHWITZ: (*To SCHIGOLCH.*) Well come on, if we're going.

SCHIGOLCH: Patience, madam. It's only a stone's throw over the Spitalstrasse. I'll be back with her in a couple of minutes.

ALVA: You're bringing her here?

SCHIGOLCH: Afraid you might catch something?

ALVA: Of course not. That ought to be obvious by now. (*He opens the centre door under the gallery.*) This way's quicker. (*SCHIGOLCH and GESCHWITZ leave the room. ALVA locks the door after them.*)

RODRIGO: You wanted to give the crazy old bat money?

ALVA: That's none of your business!

RODRIGO: And I get treated like a costermonger. In spite of my efforts to demoralise the hospital's entire nursing staff. Then there were the junior doctors and consultants...with the money I laid out on them I could've become President of the United States.

ALVA: Fraulein Geschwitz reimbursed you for every penny you paid out. My understanding is, you receive from her in addition a monthly salary of five hundred marks. Sometimes it becomes quite difficult to believe in your undying affection for our assassin.

RODRIGO: I've had more than enough of the Countess. If my bride turns into a 'company with limited liability', someone else can have her. I intend turning her into the most stunning trapeze artist, and for that I'm happy to risk my life. But in return I shall be master in my own house. I've ordered a two-inch thick hippo whip. I'm renting a fifty foot high garage to train her in. As soon as she's executed her first diving jump and not broken her neck, I'll put on my dress-suit, and never lift a finger ever again.

ALVA: Instead of which, I'm convinced that had the heroic efforts of the Countess not worked out to your advantage, you'd be lying dead drunk and penniless in a gutter somewhere,

RODRIGO: And d'you know where you'd be, if you hadn't sold off that rag your father edited for a cool two million? Teamed up with some clapped out ballerina, working as a stable-boy in Humpelmeier's Circus. What have you achieved? One thriller, in which my fiancée's legs are the two central characters, and which no respectable theatre will put on. Only two years ago I balanced two fully saddled cavalry horses on this chest.

ALVA: You? You're a...wet rag.

RODRIGO: Is that supposed to be an insult? If it is, my toecap'll hit your chin so hard, your tongue'll go walkies on the wallpaper.

ALVA: You just try it! (*Steps and voices outside.*) Who's that?

RODRIGO: It's my darling! The future most stunning trapeze artist of our time! A whole year since we've seen each other!

(*Above the staircase, the curtain parts and LULU, in a black dress and supported on SCHIGOLCH's arm, slowly makes her way down the stairs.*)

SCHIGOLCH: Come on, old girl. We've got to make it over the border today.

RODRIGO: (*Staring at LULU, stupefied.*) Hell and damnation!

LULU: (*Speaks till the end of the scene in the brightest tone.*) Easy! You're squeezing my arm!

RODRIGO: You've got a nerve, breaking out of prison with a dog like that.

SCHIGOLCH: Shut your face!

RODRIGO: I ought to fetch the police. Turn informer. A scarecrow like this thinks she can parade around in tights!

ALVA: Please, don't be insulting.

RODRIGO: Insulting you call it? I've stuffed my belly fat for these shrivelled bones. Well if I can't wangle ten thousand a year out of these shenanigans, I'm a Dutchman! Bon voyage! I'm off to the police! (*Goes.*)

SCHIGOLCH: Go then, go!

LULU: He won't dare.

SCHIGOLCH: We're best off without him. – A little black coffee for the lady! I've still got to get tickets for the sleeper.

LULU: (*Bright.*) Free at last! God's in His Heaven!

SCHIGOLCH: I'll fetch you in half an hour. We'll have our last supper in the station restaurant. – Thank you, I know every keyhole in this house.

(*Goes off through the middle door.*)

LULU: I haven't seen a proper room for a year and a half. Curtains, armchairs, pictures...

ALVA: Don't you want some coffee?

LULU: I've drunk quite enough black coffee in the past five days. Haven't you got any schnapps?

ALVA: Spa Elixir.

LULU: Brings back old times. (*As ALVA fills the glasses, she looks around the room.*) Where's my picture then?

ALVA: I put it in my room, so people wouldn't see it.

LULU: Go and fetch it.

ALVA: Even in prison you haven't lost your vanity.

LULU: It preys on your mind, you know, when you haven't looked at yourself for months. Then they gave me a brand-new dustpan. Every morning at seven, when I swept out, I'd hold the back up to my face. Hardly flattering, but it kept me happy. Shall I come with you?

(*ALVA goes off left to fetch the picture.*)

LULU: He's taken it to heart. Torturing himself fourteen months with the thought...

ALVA: (*Returning with LULU's pierrot portrait.*) It's covered in dust.

LULU: You didn't look at it while I was away?

ALVA: The Countess would've loved it in her flat, but we knew she'd be searched.

(*Lifts the picture on to the easel.*)

LULU: Now the poor dear can experience the delights of the 'Hotel Semolina' first hand.

ALVA: I still don't understand how it all came about.

LULU: Oh, the Countess worked it all out very cleverly. This summer in Hamburg there was a terrible bout of cholera. She took a course in nursing, and travelled to Hamburg to look after the cholera patients there. As soon as the opportunity arose, she put on a dead patient's underwear – they should've been burnt – and the same morning came back to see me in prison. When the warder went out, the two of us quickly changed our underclothes.

ALVA: So that's why both of you came down with cholera on the same day!

LULU: Naturally, the Countess was immediately put in the isolation ward at the hospital. And from then on she did everything she could to make us look as alike as possible. The day before yesterday she was released as cured. She returned just now and said she'd left her watch behind. I slipped her clothes on, she slipped into my prison uniform, and I walked out. (*Tickled.*) Now she's sitting over there as the murderer of Doktor Schoen.

ALVA: At least outwardly you still measure up to your picture.

LULU: My face is a bit thinner, but otherwise I'm still the same. You just get very nervy in prison.

ALVA: You looked awful as you came in.

LULU: I did that to get Jumping Jack off our backs. – And what have you been doing all this time?

ALVA: I had a critical success with a play I wrote about you.

LULU: Who's your sweetheart now?

ALVA: An actress I've rented a flat in the Karlstrasse for.

LULU: Does she love you?

ALVA: How should I know! I haven't seen her for six weeks.

LULU: And you can stand that?

ALVA: You'll never understand. My work and my sensuality are so intertwined, I'm left with the choice of either putting you in a play or making love to you.

LULU: (*As if in a dream.*) Every other night I'd dream I fell into the hands of a sex-killer. Come and give me a kiss.

ALVA: (*Kisses her.*) I have to say, your lips have got a bit thinner.

LULU: Come here! (*She pushes him into an armchair and sits on his knee.*) Am I really such a monster?

(*Kisses him passionately.*)

ALVA: Oh! Oh!

LULU: D'you remember that fancy-dress ball I went to as a page-boy? All those tipsy women running after me? The Countess kept crawling round my feet, begging me to rub my shoes in her face.

ALVA: My sweetheart, come here.

LULU: (*As if calming an unruly child.*) Sshh. I shot your father.

ALVA: I don't love you any the less for that. One kiss!

LULU: Lean your head back.

(*Kisses him very deliberately.*)

ALVA: You hold back the blaze in my heart so skilfully, you have to be the most artful seductress ever to plunge a man to his ruin.

LULU: (*Cheerful.*) If only I were! Come over the border with me. Then we can see each other as often as we wish.

ALVA: How these two slender rivals nestle together, calm in the knowledge neither will surpass the other in beauty. Until their moody mistress wakens and the two suitors part like opposite poles! – I shall sing your praises till your senses reel!

LULU: (*Laughing.*) And I will bury my hands in your hair. (*Does it.*) Will you come with me?

ALVA: Won't the old man be with you?

LULU: He won't bother us. – Is that the same divan your father bled to death on?

ALVA: Sshh.

Scene 2

A spacious salon in white stucco with wide double-doors in the rear wall, to either side of which are tall mirrors. Two doors in both side walls. Between them, to the right, a rococco console with white marble top, above which LULU's picture has been set into the wall in a narrow, gold frame. In the middle of the room a slender, brightly upholstered Louis XV sofa. Wide, brightly upholstered armchairs with thin legs and slender arms. Down left a small table. Main entrance up right. The downstage door leads to the dining-room. The middle door is open, and a wide baccarat table surrounded by Turkish upholstered chairs can be seen through it. ALVA, RODRIGO, the Marquis CASTI-PIANI, LULU, the Countess GESCHWITZ and BIANETTA move around the salon in lively conversation. The men are dressed formally. LULU wears a white, directoire-style dress with huge sleeves and lace from waist to ankles, her arms in kid gloves and her hair up with a small plume of white feathers. Countess GESCHWITZ in bright blue hussar bodice, trimmed with white fur and galooned with silver braid. White tie, a tall standing collar and stiff cuffs with huge ivory buttons. BIANETTA in dark green velvet, a wide collar of pearls, bloused sleeves, a richly pleated waistless dress, the lower hem studded with large imitation topazes set in silver.

RODRIGO: (*A full glass in his hand.*) Ladies and gentlemen…excuse me…your attention please… I drink…allow me to drink…we're here to celebrate the birthday of our gracious hostess (*Taking LULU by the arm.*) the Countess Adelaide d'Oubra…hell and damnation…therefore I drink…and so on and so forth. Ladies!
(*They all encircle LULU and clink glasses with her.*)
ALVA: (*To RODRIGO, shaking his hand.*) Congratulations.
RODRIGO: I'm sweating like a pig.
ALVA: (*To LULU.*) Shall we see if all's well in the games room?
(*They go into the gaming room.*)
BIANETTA: (*To RODRIGO.*) I'm told you're the strongest man in the world, sir.
RODRIGO: That I am, Madam. If Madam would care to see for herself –
CASTI-PIANI: (*Talks throughout the act in a bored, weary tone.*) Tell me, my dear, how come we haven't seen your charming little princess (*He gestures off.*) before today?
BIANETTA: You really find her charming? She's still at convent school. Goes back next Monday.
CASTI-PIANI: What beautiful hair she has.
RODRIGO: And look at her feet! The way she moves!

CASTI-PIANI: That's what I call breeding!

BIANETTA: Gentlemen please, have a heart! She's still just a child.

CASTI-PIANI: I wouldn't let that bother me. I'd give ten years of my life to introduce that young miss to the ways of our little cult.

BIANETTA: Well you certainly won't get my consent to that, not for a million. I'm not having her youth corrupted like mine was!

CASTI-PIANI: The confessions of a soul of generosity! Are you sure you wouldn't give your permission, even for a set of real diamonds?

BIANETTA: Stop showing off. You'd no more give my daughter diamonds than you would me. And what's more, you know it. – But, Signior Casti-Piani, tell me, d'you have any more of those Virgin shares for me?

CASTI-PIANI: Virgin shares? Ah, Madam means the *Jungfrau*. Shares in the new cable car. Well I do still have some...about four thousand, but I was keeping them for myself. The chance won't come again soon to make a quiet little fortune like that.

GESCHWITZ: I've only had a few of these Virgin shares so far. I wouldn't mind some more either.

CASTI-PIANI: I'll see what I can do, Countess. But I tell you now, you'll be paying through the nose for them. (*ALVA comes back with LULU, who remains by the door.*)

ALVA: Are we playing tonight, or not?

BIANETTA: Of course, my dear. I'm counting on it. (*To CASTI-PIANI.*) My clairvoyant's been advising me to keep my wits about me. I've got all my savings in these Virgin shares. If it doesn't come off, Signior, I'll scratch your eyes out!

CASTI-PIANI: My dear, I know exactly what I'm doing.

ALVA: I can assure you, any doubts you have are completely unfounded. I bought my *Jungfrau* shares high and don't regret it for a moment. Every day they go a little higher. There's never been anything like it.

BIANETTA: I'm glad to hear it. – As long as you're right.

ALVA: Let's take our places, shall we?

GESCHWITZ: If you'll excuse me a moment. I must speak to my friend.

ALVA: (*Offering BIANETTA his arm.*) If Madam would grant me the honour of being her partner? You have such lucky hands.

(*ALVA goes off with BIANETTA. RODRIGO scribbles something on a piece of paper and folds it together. GESCHWITZ approaches LULU by the door.*)

RODRIGO: Ah, Countess. (*GESCHWITZ starts.*) I don't look that desperate, do I? (*To himself.*) This calls for a *bon mot.* (*Aloud.*) If I may presume upon your person...

GESCHWITZ: Get lost!

CASTI-PIANI: (*Seizes the moment and takes LULU by the arm.*) A word if I may.

LULU: (*As RODRIGO surreptitiously presses his note in her hand.*) Go ahead. As many words as you want.

RODRIGO: It does me honour to excuse myself.

(*Bows and goes into the gaming room.*)

CASTI-PIANI: (*To GESCHWITZ.*) Leave us.

LULU: (*To CASTI-PIANI.*) Have I offended you in some way?

CASTI-PIANI: (*To GESCHWITZ, who hasn't moved a muscle.*) Are you deaf or what?

(*Sighing deeply, GESCHWITZ departs for the gaming-room.*)

LULU: Just tell me how much you want.

CASTI-PIANI: You can't help me with money any more.

LULU: What makes you think that?

CASTI-PIANI: Because you gave me all you had yesterday.

LULU: If you're that sure of it, you must be right.

CASTI-PIANI: You're in Queer Street, you and your writer friend.

LULU: Why beat around the bush then? If you want me to come to you, you don't need to threaten me.

CASTI-PIANI: I know. But as I told you before, it's not you I'm after. I haven't cleaned you out because I loved you. I've loved you in order to clean you out. I'd sooner have Bianetta than you. All you do is ruin a man's nervous system. Which is what makes you so suitable for the job I've found you.

LULU: Are you mad? I haven't asked you to find a job for me.

CASTI-PIANI: I told you I was in the employment business.

LULU: You told me you were a police spy.

CASTI-PIANI: You can't live off that. My colleagues are all kept by their women. It was more natural for me to resort to my former occupation. I've already helped several young things, hungry to see a bit of life, to where their talents are naturally suited.

LULU: (*Determined.*) I'm no good at that.

CASTI-PIANI: It doesn't matter what you think. The public prosecutor will pay a thousand marks to whoever turns Doktor Schoen's murderer over to the police. All I have to do is whistle down to that policeman on the corner, and I've earned a thousand marks. Against that, the Oikonomopolous Emporium in Cairo has offered me sixty pounds. That's two hundred marks more.

LULU: (*As above.*) I could never live in a place like that and be happy. When I was fifteen I was lucky enough to spend three months in hospital without setting eyes on a man. Every night in my dreams I saw the man I was created for. Ever since then I can tell at a hundred paces on a night black as hell if we'll he any good for each other. And if I go against my better judgement, I feel defiled – body and soul. And you've got the nerve to imagine I'd give myself to any Tom, Dick or Harry.

CASTI-PIANI: It isn't Tom, Dick or Harry at Oikonomopolous' place. His clientele is made up of Scottish lords, Russian dignitaries, Indian governors and dashing Rhineland industrialists. Anyway, if you don't like the man, you don't have to show him any feelings. Just get him to leave his card, and that's that!

LULU: (*Her voice quivering.*) I'm beginning to think last night's done something to your brain. I'm supposed to believe this Egyptian will pay twelve hundred francs for someone he's never set eyes on?

CASTI-PIANI: I took the liberty of sending him your picture.

LULU: The pictures I gave you!

CASTI-PIANI: I imagine he'll hang the one of you as Eve in front of a mirror outside his door.

LULU: Isn't it obvious I'd never let myself be locked away in a...house of pleasure.

CASTI-PIANI: Then you'll allow me to call the policeman.

LULU: (*Wondering.*) Why don't you just ask me for twelve hundred marks, if you need the money?

CASTI-PIANI: I don't need the money. Besides, I wouldn't ask for it because I know you're on your uppers.

LULU: We still have thirty thousand marks.

CASTI-PIANI: In *Jungfrau* shares. The prosecutor pays in currency of the Reich, and Oikonomopolous pays in English gold. You can be on board tomorrow morning. Here, you're closer to prison than anywhere. I'd be grateful for an immediate decision. The train goes at half past midnight.

LULU: You can't be serious with all this?

CASTI-PIANI: Don't you realise I'm thinking only of your safety?

LULU: I'll go with you to America, to China even. But I will not sell myself. It's worse than prison.

CASTI-PIANI: Just read this – it's straight from the heart. (*He pulls a letter from his pocket.*) There's the post-mark. Cairo. Just so you don't think I'm working with forged documents.

LULU: (*Reads, then.*) I cannot sell the only thing I can truly call my own.

CASTI-PIANI: Let me read the rest.

LULU: I'll give you everything we own. Tonight.

CASTI-PIANI: Look, believe me, I've already had your last ha'penny. If we don't leave this house by eleven you'll be transported *tout de suite* back to Germany with your whole gang.

LULU: You can't hand me over just like that!

CASTI-PIANI: You think I haven't done worse in my life? If we're travelling tonight, I'd better have a quick word with Bianetta.

73

(*CASTI-PIANI goes into the gaming room, leaving the doors open behind him. LULU stares at the floor, mechanically crumpling the note RODRIGO gave her, which she has held on to all this time. ALVA rises from the gaming table and enters, a securities note in his hand.*)

ALVA: Brilliant! It's all going brilliantly! The Countess is staking the shirt off her back, and Casti-Piani's promised me another ten *Jungfrau* shares. Even Bianetta keeps piling up her pennies.
(*Goes down right.*)

LULU: Me in a brothel?
(*Reads the note in her hand and laughs manically.*)

ALVA: (*Coming back, a cash-box in his hand.*) Aren't you going to join in?

LULU: Of course, of course! Why not?
(*ALVA returns to the gaming room. LULU is about to follow when Countess GESCHWITZ blocks her path.*)

GESCHWITZ: Are you going because I'm coming?

LULU: (*Resolute.*) No, I swear. But if you're coming I'm going.

GESCHWITZ: You've cheated me out of every earthly possession I ever had. You could at least observe the common courtesies towards me.

LULU: (*As above.*) I'm as straightforward with you as I am with any woman. I simply ask that you be the same.

GESCHWITZ: Have you forgotten the passionate declaration you made to me when we lay in that hospital together? I let myself be locked in prison for you!

LULU: And why was it necessary to give me cholera first? (*Pause.*) Throughout that whole business I promised myself things quite different from what I was forced to promise you. It fills me with horror to think they might ever come true.

GESCHWITZ: So you were cheating me from the start?

LULU: (*Brightly.*) What have you been cheated out of? Your physical charms have found such an enthusiastic admirer here I'm wondering how I shall ever make ends meet. I shall have to go back to piano-teaching. A seventeen-year-old couldn't make the poor man more infatuated than you have with your contrariness, you monster!

GESCHWITZ: Who do you mean? I don't understand.

LULU: (*As above.*) I mean your acrobat, Rodrigo Quast. What a muscle-man. He balances two saddled cavalry horses on his chest. What woman could wish for anything more wonderful? Just a moment ago he told me he'll throw himself in the river if you won't take pity on him.

GESCHWITZ: I don't envy your skill at sacrificing the helpless victims inscrutable fate has delivered into your hands. I feel as free as a goddess when I think of the animals you've become enslaved to.

LULU: Who are you talking about?

GESCHWITZ: Casti-Piani. The basest depravity is written on his forehead in inch-high letters.

LULU: That's enough! Say one bad thing about him and I'll kick you. He gives me proofs of his altruism which only now have revealed to me how abominable you are. You remained unformed in the womb, neither man nor woman. Too little matter for a man, and too much brain for a woman. That's why you're cracked! Try Fraulein Bianetta. She'll have anyone if the price is right. (*ALVA, CASTI-PIANI, RODRIGO and BIANETTA come in from the gaming room.*) My goodness, has something happened?

CASTI-PIANI: Nothing at all. We're thirsty, that's all.

BIANETTA: Everyone's won! I can't believe it. I seem to have won a fortune.

ALVA: Don't get too excited, it brings bad luck.

CASTI-PIANI: Ours not to reason why. All we need to know is, we don't have to stint on champagne!

BIANETTA: (*To CASTI-PIANI.*) I can even afford a meal in a decent restaurant afterwards.

ALVA: Meanwhile we have a buffet! Ladies, this way! (*They all go into the dining-room. RODRIGO holds LULU back.*)

RODRIGO: One moment, my dear. – Did you read my billet-doux?

LULU: You can threaten to rat on me all you like. I just
haven't got the money.

RODRIGO: Don't lie to me, you trollop! You've still got
forty thousand in *Jungfrau* shares. Your so-called husband
has been parading them around.

LULU: Why don't you try him then?

RODRIGO: Thanks a lot. I could spend a week explaining
it to that dimwit and he still wouldn't understand the
score. Meanwhile my intended writes 'we're finished',
and I'm back working a barrel-organ.

LULU: You mean you've got engaged here?

RODRIGO: I suppose you think I should've got your
permission first. What thanks did I get for getting you
out of prison? I'd be a coolie by now if this girl hadn't
taken me in hand. This country's going to the dogs. If I'd
been a boxing kangaroo, I'd have had my picture in all
the newspapers. Thank God I knew Celestine from way
back. She's got twenty years savings in the bank. And
what's more, she loves me for myself. She's got three
kids by an American bishop, and they've all got great
expectations.

LULU: My blessings go with you.

RODRIGO: You know what you can do with your blessings.
I told her I'd got twenty thousand in the bank in
securities.

LULU: (*Chuffed.*) And he says she loves him for himself!

RODRIGO: My Celestine respects the spiritual side of me,
not the muscleman, like you and all the others. I'd
sooner be a corpse than let myself in for those fun and
games again!

LULU: So why on earth are you following poor Geschwitz
around with your endless propositions?

RODRIGO: Because she's a nob. After all, I'm a man of the
world. I can hold my own better than any of you in the
most refined conversation. But just now I've had chit-
chat up to here. Will you get the money for me by
tomorrow evening or not?

LULU: I haven't got any money.

RODRIGO: What d'you think I've got for brains? Chicken-shit? He'd give you the shirt off his back if you'd only do your conjugal duty by him! You'll make four people happy if you stop nitpicking and sacrifice yourself to this one good deed! Must it be Casti-Piani for always and ever?

LULU: (*Cheerful.*) Shall I ask him to show you the way downstairs?

RODRIGO: It's up to you, Countess. If I haven't got the twenty thousand by tomorrow evening, I'll tell the police and all this holding court will be over for ever. – Goodbye!

(*LULU goes off into the dining room. RODRIGO follows her. CASTI-PIANI comes on from the gaming room.*)

CASTI-PIANI: Things are hotting up. If I don't slit your throat, you slit mine.

(*BOB, a fifteen year-old hotel boy in a red jacket, tight leather trousers and tall, shiny boots enters with a telegram.*)

BOB: Mr Casti-Piani.

(*CASTI-PIANI breaks open the telegram. BOB proceeds to the dining-room.*)

CASTI-PIANI: (*Mutters.*) *Jungfrau* Cable-Car shares fallen to…' Well, what'd you expect? (*He puts the telegram away as BOB returns, bringing LULU behind him.*) Wait! (*Gives BOB a tip. As he goes, to LULU.*) Look at those trousers! God almighty! I can't take all this.

(*He goes into the dining room. BOB comes back almost immediately, bringing SCHIGOLCH in tail-coat, a white tie, trodden-down patent shoes and a shabby top hat, which he holds on to.*)

SCHIGOLCH: (*Glancing at BOB as he goes.*) Where'd you get him from?

LULU: The circus.

SCHIGOLCH: How d'you pay him?

LULU: Ask him if you're that concerned.

SCHIGOLCH: (*Sitting.*) Fact of the matter is, I need money myself. I've rented a room for my girlfriend.

LULU: You've got a lover here too!

SCHIGOLCH: She's from Frankfurt. She was the King of Naples' wife in her youth. Every day she tells me how seductive she used to be.

LULU: (*Seemingly in total control.*) Does she need the money very badly?

SCHIGOLCH: She'd like to set herself up in a little flat. Money like that doesn't matter to you, does it?

LULU: (*Suddenly seized by a fit of weeping, falls to SCHIGOLCH's feet.*) Oh my God!

SCHIGOLCH: (*Stroking her.*) What's all this? What's the matter then?

LULU: (*Gulps convulsively.*) It's too too awful!

SCHIGOLCH: (*Pulls her on his knee and holds her in his arms like a child.*) There there…you're overdoing it, my girl… You need to go to bed with a good book – for a change. Go on. Cry it all out… I remember it taking you like this when you were fifteen. No one ever howled like you'd howl in those days… And you didn't wear see-through stockings then either.

LULU: (*Howling.*) Take me home with you! Take me tonight! Please! There are plenty of cabs down there.

SCHIGOLCH: I'll take you. I'll take you. – But what's the matter?

LULU: My head's on the block! They're going to rat on me!

SCHIGOLCH: Who? Who's ratting on you?

LULU: Jumping Jack.

SCHIGOLCH: (*With utmost calm.*) I'll take care of him.

LULU: (*Pleading.*) Oh yes, take care of him! Please, take care of him! Then do with me what you want!

SCHIGOLCH: Send him to me and he's had it. My window looks over the river. But (*He shakes his head.*) he won't come, will he.

LULU: What number are you?

SCHIGOLCH: 376, last house before the Hippodrome.

LULU: I'll send him to you. He'll come with that crazy woman who's always crawling round my feet. He'll come tonight. Get back there now and make it nice.

SCHIGOLCH: Just send 'em to me. – And then, my girl? And then?

LULU: I'll give you the money for your sweetheart.

SCHIGOLCH: That's a bit mean.

LULU: And anything you want! All I've got!

SCHIGOLCH: Soon it'll be ten years since we've known each other.

LULU: Is that all you're after? But you've got her, haven't you?

SCHIGOLCH: My Frankfurter's seen better days.

LULU: Then swear to me!

SCHIGOLCH: Have I ever let you down?

LULU: Swear to me you'll take care of him.

SCHIGOLCH: I'll take care of him.

LULU: Swear it! Swear it!

SCHIGOLCH: (*Puts his hand on her ankle.*) By everything that's holy. When he comes tonight –

LULU: How cooling that is!

SCHIGOLCH: Like a furnace.

LULU: Go straight home then. They'll be there in half an hour. Take a cab.

SCHIGOLCH: I'm going, I'm going.

LULU: Quick! Please! Good God...

SCHIGOLCH: What are you looking at me like that for?

LULU: My garter's undone.

SCHIGOLCH: So what? – is there something else?

LULU: It's bad luck.

SCHIGOLCH: (*Yawning.*) Not for you, my girl. Don't worry. I'll take care of him.

> (*He goes. LULU props her left foot on a stool, ties her garter and goes into the gaming room. RODRIGO is jostled out of the dining-room by CASTI-PIANI.*)

RODRIGO: You could at least treat me decently.

CASTI-PIANI: (*Totally unconcerned.*) Why on earth should I? I want to know what you were talking about with her just now.

RODRIGO: In that case you know what you can do.

CASTI-PIANI: Are you going to give me a straight answer or not! You were insisting she go up with you in the lift.

RODRIGO: That is a disgusting, perfidious lie!

CASTI-PIANI: She told me herself! You threatened to denounce her if she didn't go with you.

RODRIGO: If I wanted her for myself, God knows I wouldn't have to threaten her with prison first.

CASTI-PIANI: Thank you. That's all I wanted to know. (*Goes through the main door.*)

RODRIGO: What a swine! I should've thrown him at the ceiling so he stuck there – like a Limberger cheese. Or better still, strangled him with his own guts.

LULU: (*Coming from the dining-room, jolly.*) Where've you been? I've been looking everywhere.

RODRIGO: I showed him. You don't mess with me.

LULU: Showed who?

RODRIGO: Your Casti-Piani friend! How could you tell him I tried to seduce you, you tart?

LULU: I seem to remember someone demanding I give myself to my dead husband's son for twenty thousand marks in *Jungfrau* shares.

RODRIGO: Because it's your duty to take pity on the poor boy! You blasted his father away, in front of his eyes, in his prime. – But I tell you, this Casti-Piani of yours will think twice before he crosses my path again.

LULU: The Countess is in a terrible state. She'll throw herself in the river if you leave her waiting any longer.

RODRIGO: What's the cow waiting for then?

LULU: For you to take her with you.

RODRIGO: Then give her my compliments and tell her to jump.

LULU: She'll lend me twenty thousand marks to save me from ruin if you'll save her from it herself. If you take her with you tonight, I'll deposit twenty thousand in any bank of your choosing.

RODRIGO: And if I don't?

LULU: Then turn me in. Alva and I are broke.

RODRIGO: Hell and damnation.

LULU: You'll make four people happy if you stop nitpicking and sacrifice yourself to this one good deed.

RODRIGO: It won't work. I know. I've tried it enough times already. I was such a gentleman you wouldn't have thought I was in show business at all.

LULU: (*Trying it on.*) She's still a virgin.

RODRIGO: (*Sighs.*) I just hope there's a God in Heaven. To pay you back for all these cracks of yours.

LULU: She's walting. What shall I say?

RODRIGO: Give her my respects and tell her I'm a pervert.

LULU: I'll tell her now.

RODRIGO: Wait! – I'll definitely get the twenty thousand from her?

LULU: Ask her yourself!

RODRIGO: Then tell her I'm ready. I'll wait for her in the dining-room. First I have to see about a tub of caviar. (*He goes into the dining room. LULU opens the door to the gaming room and calls 'Martha!' brightly. GESCHWITZ steps into the salon and shuts the door behind her.*)

LULU: (*Pleased.*) My dearest, you have the chance to save me from a fate worse than death.

GESCHWITZ: Just tell me how.

LULU: By going to a boarding-house with Jumping Jack.

GESCHWITZ: Why, my dear?

LULU: He's saying you must be his tonight, or he'll turn me in tomorrow.

GESCHWITZ: You know I can't belong to any man. It's my destiny not to.

LULU: If he doesn't like you, that's his own look-out. Why fall for you in the first place!

GESCHWITZ: But he'll be a brute. He'll make up for his disappointment by smashing my skull. It wouldn't be the first time. Couldn't you spare me this once?

LULU: What good would it do you, if he turned me in?

GESCHWITZ: I still have enough put by for the two of us to travel to America – only second-class, I'm afraid. But at least there you'd be free of all your pursuers.

LULU: (*Cheerful.*) I want to stay. I couldn't be happier anywhere else. You have to tell him you can't live without him. He'll be flattered and go quiet as a lamb. Give the coachman this note: it's got the address on it. Number 376 is a fifth-rate hotel, and they're expecting you tonight.

GESCHWITZ: How can such a horrendous thing save you? I don't understand. You've conjured up the worst possible torture for an outcast like me.

LULU: Perhaps the encounter will cure you!

GESCHWITZ: (*Sighs.*) Oh Lulu, if there is retribution in eternity, I shouldn't like to be your stand-in! I can't accept a God doesn't watch over us, yet I'm sure you're right it does us no good. Why else should an insignificant worm like me endure only horror when the whole of living creation seems out of its mind with bliss!

LULU: Why complain? When you do find happiness, you'll be a hundred-thousand times happier than any of we ordinary mortals ever will.

GESCHWITZ: I know that, and I envy no one. But I'm still waiting. You've betrayed me so often already.

LULU: My darling, I'm yours, if you will pacify this Jumping Jack till tomorrow. It's only his vanity needs appeasing. You must beg him to take pity on you.

GESCHWITZ: And tomorrow?

LULU: I'll be waiting for you, my sweet. I shan't receive anyone – not even the hairdresser – I shan't open my eyes till you come and are with me.

GESCHWITZ: Then have him come in.

LULU: But you must fling yourself at him, my darling! D'you still have the number?

GESCHWITZ: 376. Just get on with it!

LULU: (*Calls into the dining-room.*) D'you have a moment, my dear?

RODRIGO: (*Coming out of the dining-room.*) Excuse me having my mouth full, ladies.

GESCHWITZ: (*Grabs his hands.*) I adore you! Take pity on my need!

RODRIGO: Here we go! Into the breach!
(*He offers GESCHWITZ his arm and leaves the salon with her.*)

LULU: Goodnight, my little ones. (*She accompanies the couple out into the corridor and comes back immediately with BOB.*) Quickly, Bob, quickly! We have to leave at once. You're coming with me. But we must swop clothes.

BOB: (*Bright.*) Whatever madam says.

LULU: What's all this 'madam' business? You're giving me
your clothes and getting into mine. Come on!
(*They go off into the dining room. A noise breaks out in the
gaming room, and the doors are flung open. ALVA, CASTI-
PIANI and BIANETTA come into the salon.*)

ALVA: (*His securities in his hand.*) You can accept these
Jungfrau securities, can't you?

CASTI-PIANI: They're not worth the paper they're written
on.

BIANETTA: You crook! You don't want me to get my own
back, that's all!

CASTI-PIANI: I'm not giving up the game, I just want
cash. This isn't the Exchange, you know. He can give me
his scrap of paper tomorrow.

ALVA: A scrap you call it? My understanding is these
shares are standing at 210.

CASTI-PIANI: Yesterday they were at 210. Today they're
nowhere. And tomorrow you won't find anything
cheaper or more tasteful to paper your hall.

ALVA: But how come! – This means we're all up the creek!
(*Sits heavily.*)

CASTI-PIANI: That's right. And tomorrow I shall resume
the struggle for a secure existence for only the thirty-
sixth time!

BIANETTA: But have I got this right? *Jungfrau* shares have
fallen?

CASTI-PIANI: Even further than you, madam. You could
get more for them to use as hair-curlers.

BIANETTA: Oh my good God! Ten years' work. (*She
swoons. CASTI-PIANI catches her.*) Tell me, Signior, now
your entire fortune has gone, where are you thinking of
eating this evening?

CASTI-PIANI: Wherever you wish, my dear. Take me
wherever you want. But make it quick. Things are
hotting up round here.

BIANETTA: There's a little place open all night. D'you
know 'The Five-legged Calf'? Perhaps by morning we
could sort something out.

CASTI-PIANI: Don't you ever sleep then?

BIANETTA: Well of course. But never at night. – Kadidya! Where is that girl?

(*BIANETTA and CASTI-PIANI leave by the main door. LULU enters from the dining room dressed in BOB's costume plus jockey-cap and travelling cloak.*)

LULU: D'you still have some cash, Alva?

ALVA: (*Looking up.*) Are you mad?

LULU: The police'll be here in two minutes. We've been shopped. You can stay if you want.

ALVA: (*Jumping up.*) Lord have mercy!

(*Knocking on a door offstage. They leave by a side door. We hear the voices of a police officer and CASTI-PIANI off.*)

VOICE: (*Off.*) I arrest you madam, in the name of the law!

CASTI-PIANI: But, officer, what are you doing? This is the wrong woman!

Scene 3

An attic room with no gable-windows. Two large skylights in the slope of the roof open upwards. Down left and right two badly fitting doors. A torn grey mattress on the right fore-stage. Down left a wobbly flower stand, on which are a bottle and a smoking paraffin lamp. An old chaise-longue upstage left in the corner. A cane chair with a broken seat near the centre door. Rain can be heard on the roof. A bowl full of water stands underneath the hole in the roof. SCHIGOLCH lies on the mattress in a long grey overcoat. ALVA lies on the chaise-longue, wrapped in a rug, the straps of which hang above him from the wall.

SCHIGOLCH: The rain's playing reveille.

ALVA: It's setting the mood for her debut! (*Pause.*) I just dreamed we were having dinner together in the Olympia rooms. Bianetta was still with us. The tablecloth was dripping champagne from all four corners.

SCHIGOLCH: Yeh, yeh…and I dreamed of Christmas pudding.

(*LULU, her hair falling to her shoulders, appears barefoot downstage right, in a shabby black dress.*)

SCHIGOLCH: Where've you been, my girl?

LULU: I wouldn't mind if I could warm up a bit on one of you two.

SCHIGOLCH: There's always a lot of moaning to start with. She was just the same twenty years ago.

ALVA: The bowl's running over.

SCHIGOLCH: You'll miss the office workers going home after dinner.

LULU: If I could lie somewhere I'm not woken by a kick!

ALVA: Me too. Why let things drag on like this? I'd sooner we starved to death together in peace this very night. Let's face it, we've reached the end of the line.

LULU: Why don't you go and get us something to eat then? You've never earned a penny in your life.

ALVA: In this weather? You wouldn't chase a dog out of doors in this.

LULU: But you'll chase me! I'm supposed to give the last drop of blood in my veins so you can stuff your faces.

ALVA: I won't touch a farthing of the money.

SCHIGOLCH: Just let her go. All I want is one more Christmas pudding, then I'll have had enough. – She'd sooner see us perish in front of her eyes than do us this one little favour.

LULU: If you hadn't sold my clothes, then at least I wouldn't have to avoid the lamplight. I'd like to see the woman who could earn a bean in the rags I've got on.

ALVA: I've tried everything humanly possible. All the time I had money I spent whole nights working out systems which should've won even against the most perfect card-sharp. And still I lost.

SCHIGOLCH: Yeh, yeh… Couldn't you finally get your skates on, my dear? I've got a feeling I won't get much older in this place. I've had no feeling in my toes for months. Later on, I'd like to drink a few whiskies in the pub downstairs. The landlady told me yesterday I still had a serious chance of becoming her lover.

LULU: All right all right all right! I'll go down.

(*She takes the bottle from the table and drinks.*)

85

SCHIGOLCH: Just so they can smell you coming a mile off.

LULU: I'm not drinking it all.

ALVA: You're not going down there! You're my wife! I forbid it!

LULU: How can you forbid anything when you can't even feed yourself!

ALVA: Whose fault is that? My wife has put me in this sickbed – no one else.

LULU: Am I sick?

ALVA: Who dragged me through the mire? Who turned me into my father's murderer?

LULU: Did you shoot him? He didn't have a lot to lose, but when I see you lying there, I could chop my hands off for sinning against my better judgement.
(*She goes off right to her room.*)

ALVA: She gave it me from Casti-Piani. She should've been born Empress of Russia. Then she'd have found her level. A second Catherine the Second.

LULU: (*Coming back from her room carrying a pair of ankle boots, and sitting on the floor to put them on.*) As long as I don't go arse-over-tip down the stairs. – Huah, it's cold. Is there anything sadder in this world than a woman of pleasure?

SCHIGOLCH: Give it time, give it time. All it needs is one lucky break.

LULU: Fine by me. Nothing worse can happen to me now. (*She puts the bottle to her lips.*) It warms you up. – Oh hell! (*Goes off through the centre door.*)

SCHIGOLCH: Soon as we hear her coming back, we'd better creep in my hidey-hole.

ALVA: When I think back…we were like brother and sister at the start. I came across her by chance one morning, getting dressed. Doktor Goll had been called for a consultation. Her hairdresser had read my first poem… And then she came to the ball at the Spanish Embassy. It was almost as if Doktor Goll had a premonition of his death. He asked me to dance with her, so she wouldn't do anything stupid. Papa never took his eyes off us. And all through the waltzes she stared at him over my shoulder.

SCHIGOLCH: I'm just afraid no one will bite now.

ALVA: Though she was already a full-grown woman, she had the look of a breezy, rosy-cheeked five-year-old.

SCHIGOLCH: Just so long as she doesn't panic with the respectable ones and bring back some tramp she's been swopping true confessions with.

ALVA: She was in her bridal gown the first time I kissed her. But she refused to remember it afterwards. Even so, I'm sure that, even in my father's arms I stood between her and her conscience. That's also how she acquired her terrible power over me.

SCHIGOLCH: They're here!

(*The sound of heavy footsteps on the staircase.*)

ALVA: (*Jumping up.*) I won't go through with it! I'll throw the man out!

SCHIGOLCH: (*Pulls himself up painfully, takes ALVA by the collar and bundles him left.*) Come on, quick march! How's the fella going to unburden his soul if the two of us are hanging around?

ALVA: But what if he makes improper suggestions?

SCHIGOLCH: What if he does! What else is he going to say? He's only human.

ALVA: Let's leave the door open.

SCHIGOLCH: (*Pushing ALVA into the hiding-place.*) Don't be stupid! – Get down!

ALVA: (*Inside.*) He'd better watch out, that's all.

(*LULU opens the centre door and ushers in Mr HUNIDEI. He's a man of hen-like appearance, smoothly shaven with pink cheeks, bright blue eyes and a friendly smile. He wears a top hat, a cape and carries a dripping umbrella in his hand.*)

LULU: This is where I live. (*HUNIDEI puts his index finger to his lips and looks at LULU meaningfully. Then he opens his umbrella and puts it upstage on the floor to dry.*) It's not exactly the Ritz, of course. (*HUNIDEI comes down to her and holds her hand over her mouth.*) What are you trying to say? (*HUNIDEI holds her hand to her mouth and puts his*

index finger to his lips.) I don't know what you mean.
(*HUNIDEI quickly holds her mouth shut. LULU, escaping.*)
We're quite alone here. No one can hear us. (*HUNIDEI
holds his finger to his lips, shakes his head to say no, points to
LULU, opens his mouth as if to speak, points to himself and
then to the doors. LULU, to herself.*) My God – he's off his
head!
(*HUNIDEI holds her mouth shut. Then goes upstage, folds
his cape up and lays it over the chair near the door. Then he
comes downstage, grinning, takes her head in both hands and
kisses her forehead.*)

SCHIGOLCH: (*Behind the half-open door down left.*) This
one's got a screw loose.

ALVA: He'd better watch our, that's all!

SCHIGOLCH: She couldn't have found anyone more
dismal if she'd tried.

LULU: (*Backing off.*) Are you going to give me a little
something? (*HUNIDEI puts his hand over her mouth and
presses a gold coin in her hand. LULU inspects the coin and
throws it from one hand to the other. HUNIDEI looks at her
questioningly.*) All right, that'll do. (*She puts the money in
her pocket. HUNIDEI quickly puts his hand over her mouth,
gives her a few silver coins and throws her a peremptory
glance.*) Well, that's very nice of you!
(*HUNIDEI jumps around the room wildly, waving his arms
in the air and gazes desperately into the sky. LULU approaches
him cautiously, throws her arm round his neck and kisses him
on the mouth. HUNIDEI, laughing silently, frees himself
from her and looks around questioningly. LULU takes the
lamp from the flower stand and opens the door to her room.
HUNIDEI steps in, smiling and lifting his hat as he goes
through the door. The room is dark, except for a beam of light
coming through the bedroom door. ALVA and SCHIGOLCH
creep out of their hiding-place on all fours.*)

ALVA: Have they gone or what?

SCHIGOLCH: (*Behind him.*) Wait a minute.

ALVA: I can't hear a thing here.

SCHIGOLCH: You've heard that often enough!

ALVA: I'm going to kneel by her door.

SCHIGOLCH: God, what a mummy's boy. (*He presses past ALVA, feels his way across the stage, picks Mr HUNIDEI's cape up from the chair and goes through its pockets. ALVA has crept over to LULU's door.*) Gloves, that's all. (*He turns the cape over, goes through the inside pockets and pulls out a book which he gives to ALVA.*) See what that is.

ALVA: (*Holds the book up to the beam of light coming from the bedroom and slowly deciphers the title page.*) 'Exhortations to Pious Pilgrims and those Aspiring to the Same.' – A fat help! Price two shillings and sixpence.

SCHIGOLCH: He looks totally God-forsaken to me. (*Lays the coat back over the chair and feels his way back to the hiding place.*) They've had it, these people. Their glory days are all in the past. The man hasn't even got a silk scarf.

ALVA: (*ALVA making his way back.*) Come on, let's get out of sight.

SCHIGOLCH: All she does is think of herself and take the first one to come along. I hope the bastard realises he's getting the time of his life.

(*They creep back into their hiding place and close the doors after them. Then LULU comes in and puts the lamp back on the flower stand.*)

LULU: Will you come and see me again?

(*HUNIDEI puts his hand over her mouth. LULU looks skyward in desperation and shakes her head. HUNIDEI has put his cape round his shoulders and approaches her with his grinning smile. She throws herself round his neck, whereupon he quietly frees himself, kisses her hand and turns towards the door. She goes to accompany him, but he motions her to stay back and silently leaves the room. SCHIGOLCH and ALVA come out of hiding.*)

LULU: (*Dead.*) God, he gave me the willies.

ALVA: How much'd he give you?

LULU: (*The same.*) Here's the lot. Take it. I'm going back down.

SCHIGOLCH: We could live like kings up here.

ALVA: He's coming back.

SCHIGOLCH: We'd better get back then.

ALVA: He must be looking for his prayer-book. Here it is. It must've fallen out of his coat.

LULU: (*Listening.*) No, it's not him. It's someone else. – Who could it be?

SCHIGOLCH: He's probably recommended us to a friend. – Come in!

(*Countess GESCHWITZ comes in. She's poorly dressed and carries a rolled-up canvas under her arms.*)

GESCHWITZ: If I've come at a bad time, I'll go back. I have to say, I haven't talked to a living soul for ten days. And I have to tell you straight away, I haven't laid hands on any money. My brother didn't even answer.

SCHIGOLCH: And now her Grace has come to grace us with her presence?

LULU: (*Dead.*) I'm going back down.

GESCHWITZ: Where d'you think you're going dressed like that? I haven't come entirely empty-handed. A tinker offered me twelve shillings for it on my way here. But I couldn't bear to part with it. You can sell it if you like.

SCHIGOLCH: What is it?

ALVA: Let me see. (*He takes the canvas from her and unrolls it, visibly delighted.*) Oh my goodness, look, it's Lulu's portrait!

LULU: (*Screaming.*) You bring that here, you monster? Take it out of my sight! Throw it out the window!

ALVA: (*Suddenly re-invigorated, delighted.*) What's wrong? Just seeing this portrait again brings back my self-respect. Helps me understand what's happened to me. Everything we've been through is as clear as day. (*Somewhat elegaic.*) Any man who can look at those full blooming lips, those big innocent eyes, and that rosy-white body bursting with life and still feel secure in his bourgeois attitudes, let him cast the first stone.

SCHIGOLCH: We must hang it up. It'll make a big impression on our clientele.

ALVA: Leave it to me. I know how to do it.

(*He tugs several nails from the wall, pulls off his left boot and knocks the nails through the corners of the picture into the wall.*)

SCHIGOLCH: How did you come by it?

GESCHWITZ: I cut it down from the wall of your flat after you left.

SCHIGOLCH: It needs to hang a while to really come into its own.

GESCHWITZ: It must've been an eminently gifted artist who painted it.

LULU: (*Calm again, approaches the picture with the lamp.*) You didn't know him then?

GESCHWITZ: No. It must've been before my time. I only heard you mention disparagingly from time to time that he was paranoid and cut his throat.

ALVA: (*Comparing the portrait with LULU.*) The childlike expression in the eyes is still the same – in spite of everything. (*Blithely.*) Thank God you don't notice how people deteriorate when you're with them every day.

SCHIGOLCH: Down there in the lamplight she could hold her own with a dozen creatures of the night.

LULU: (*As pleased as ALVA.*) I'll go and see if you're right. – Cheers.

ALVA: (*In impetuous anger.*) You're not going back down as long as I live!

GESCHWITZ: Where are you going?

ALVA: She wants to bring a man up.

GESCHWITZ: Lulu!

ALVA: She's already done it once this evening.

GESCHWITZ: Lulu, Lulu, where you go, I go too!

SCHIGOLCH: If you're hoping to make a few bob, I'd suggest you find a beat of your own.

GESCHWITZ: Lulu, I shan't leave your side. I'm armed.

SCHIGOLCH: Godammit to hell! Now Her Grace is muscling in on our bait!

LULU: You'll he the death of me, all of you! I can't stand it here any longer!

GESCHWITZ: You have nothing to fear! I'll stand by you!

(*LULU goes off with GESCHWITZ through the middle door.*)

SCHIGOLCH: Damn and blast!

ALVA: (*Throwing himself on his chaise-longue and whining.*) I've a feeling I can't hope for much more from this world.

SCHIGOLCH: We should've held the damn woman back by the throat. Any life or hope, she'll drive it away with that aristocratic skull of hers. – Having said that, she's got more guts than ten men put together. If she hadn't enticed Jumping Jack to my place that time we'd still have him on our backs today. Could you turn the lamp up a bit?

ALVA: My God, what have I done with my life?

SCHIGOLCH: What's this damn weather done to my raincoat. I looked after myself better when I was twenty-five.

ALVA: No one could've pursued with greater single-mindedness than I the company of people who'd never read a book in their lives. I latched on to these people with total enthusiasm and self-denial, in order to be carried to the greatest heights of poetic fame. But I miscalculated. I'm a martyr to my profession. Since the death of my father I haven't written a single verse.

SCHIGOLCH: They're coming back! – We'd better hide again.

ALVA: I'm staying here. (*Hides under his rug.*)

SCHIGOLCH: Why d'you feel so sorry for her? They pays their money, they takes their choice.
(*Retreats to his hiding place.*)

ALVA: I no longer have the moral courage to put myself out for mere money.

LULU: (*Opening the door.*) Come on in, dearie.
(*KUNGU POTI, heir to the kingdom of Uahubee enters, in a brightly coloured topcoat, bright trousers, white gaiters, yellow-buttoned boots and a grey top-hat. His speech is characterised by the typically African sibilants and is interrupted by frequent belching.*)

KUNGU POTI: Goddam staircase dark.

LULU: It's lighter in here, my love. (*Taking his hand and bringing him downstage.*) Come on, come on!

KUNGU POTI: But cold in here. Damn cold.

LULU: D'you want a whisky?

KUNGU POTI: Whisky? I always drink whisky. Whisky damn good.

LULU: (*Gives him the bottle.*) I don't know where the glass has got to.

KUNGU POTI: No matter. (*Drinks from the bottle.*) Whisky! Much whisky!

LULU: You're a fine young man.

KUNGU POTI: My father is Emperor of Uahubee. Over here I have six wives: two Spanish, two English, two French.

LULU: How much are you going to give me then, dearie?

KUNGU POTI: A gold sovereign! Please believe, you will have gold sovereign! Always give gold sovereign.

LULU: You can give it me later. But can I see it?

KUNGU POTI: I never pay before.

LULU: But you can show it me.

KUNGU POTI: No understand! No understand! – Come, Ragap-sishimulara! (*Grabs LULU round the waist.*) Come!

LULU: (*Struggling with all her might.*) Let me go! Let me go! (*ALVA has struggled to his feet and, creeping up behind KUNGU POTI, now pulls him off by his coat collar.*)

KUNGU POTI: (*Turning quickly to face ALVA.*) Oh! Oh! Here vipers' den! – Come, friend, you get sedative! (*He strikes ALVA with a lead-handled stick, whereupon ALVA groans and collapses.*) Here, have sleeping drops! Have opium! Sweet dreams! (*He kisses LULU and points to ALVA.*) He dream of you, Ragap-sishi-mulara! Sweet dreams!

(*Hurrying to the door and goes.*)

LULU: I'm not staying here a moment longer! – How can anyone stand it! – I'd sooner be back on the street! (*She goes. SCHIGOLCH comes out of hiding and bends over ALVA.*)

SCHIGOLCH: Blood…Alva! I'll have to get him out of the way. Hup! Or our clientele will turn up their noses…

Alva! Alva! What comes of not sorting yourself out. Got to be one thing or the other – or before long it's too late. (*He strikes a match and sticks it under ALVA's nose. When he doesn't stir.*) He wants to sleep on. Well you can't lie in here! (*He drags him by the scruff of the neck into LULU's bedroom, then tries to turn the lamp up.*) I'd better get going, or I'll miss my Christmas pud. (*Catches sight of LULU's picture.*) She'll never get the hang of this game. How can you live off love when love is your life? – She's coming back. I'll appeal to her conscience.

(*The door opens and Countess GESCHWITZ enters.*)

SCHIGOLCH: If you're thinking of kipping down for the night with us, make sure nothing's stolen, would you?

GESCHWITZ: It's black in here!

SCHIGOLCH: It'll get a lot blacker, believe me. – The Herr Doktor is having a lie-down.

GESCHWITZ: She sent me on ahead.

SCHIGOLCH: Very sensible. – If anyone asks after me, I'm downstairs in the pub. (*Goes.*)

GESCHWITZ: I'll sit by the door. I want to see everything and not bat an eyelid. (*Sits in the straw armchair by the door.*) Funny how hunger robs you of the urge to be unhappy. The moment your belly's full you turn the world into a torture chamber. You can throw your whole life away on a whim. But what's happiness anyway? Sleeping better, forgetting your cares? Thank you, Lord, for not making me like that. (*She takes a small black revolver from her pocket and holds it to her temple.*) Come, my love… (*She lowers the revolver.*) Hanging would be better. If she sees me lying in blood, she won't weep for me. I was never more than a tool, willing to be used for the most irksome tasks. I've been abhorrent to her from the first day we met. How often I've dreamed of her kissing me! (*Suddenly jumping up.*) That's it! Quick, before she comes back! (*She takes the rug straps from the wall, stands on the chair, ties them to a hook in the door-post, ties the straps around her neck, kicks the chair away and falls to the ground.*) Bloody life! Let me speak to you heart-to-heart just once more, my angel! (*Drags herself in front of LULU's picture, sinks to her knees and folds her hands together.*) I should've been happy just once. My love! Have mercy on me!

(*LULU opens the door and ushers in JACK. He's a man of stocky build, fluent movements, a pale face, fiery eyes, thick and highly arched eyebrows, a drooping moustache and thin beard, shaggy side-whiskers and blood-red hands with gnawed nails. His gaze is fixed to the floor. He wears a dark overcoat and a small, rounded felt hat.*)

JACK: Who's that?

LULU: That's my sister, sir. She's mad. I don't know how to get rid of her.

JACK: You look like you got a nice mouth.

LULU: I get it from my mother.

JACK: Looks it. – How much d'you want? – I haven't got much on me.

LULU: Wouldn't you like to stay the whole night?

JACK: No, I can't. I have to go home.

LULU: You can go home tomorrow, can't you? Say you missed the last bus and had to stay with a friend.

JACK: How much d'you want?

LULU: Not a fortune in gold. – Well, maybe just a bit.

JACK: (*Turns to the door.*) Goodnight!

LULU: (*Holding him back.*) No, no. Stay for God's sake!

JACK: (*Walks past GESCHWITZ and opens the partition door.*) Why should I stay till morning? Sounds dodgy to me. While I'm asleep, someone might go through my pockets.

LULU: No, I wouldn't do that. No one would. Don't go because of that. I beg you!

JACK: How much d'you want?

LULU: All right, give me half what I said.

JACK: No, it's too much. – You not been at this game long?

LULU: Today's my first day. (*GESCHWITZ, still on her knees, has risen half up against JACK, and now LULU pulls her back by the straps which are still round her neck.*) Get down.

JACK: Leave her alone. That's not your sister. She's in love with you. (*He strokes GESCHWITZ's head like a dog.*) Poor thing.

LULU: What are you looking at me like that for?

JACK: I'm trying to judge from the way you walk. I reckon you must be built all right.

LULU: How can you tell?

JACK: I could even tell you had a nice mouth. – But all I've got on me's half-a-crown.

LULU: Well, what's the difference. – Give it me then!

JACK: But you've got to give me half back, so I can get the bus tomorrow morning.

LULU: I've got nothing in my bag.

JACK: Have a look, make sure. Go through your pockets. – There, you see what's that? Let me see!

LULU: (*Holds her hand out.*) That's all I've got.

JACK: Give me the coin.

LULU: I'll change it tomorrow morning and give you half.

JACK: No, I want all of it.

LULU: (*Gives it him.*) Jesus Christ! – Come on then! (*Takes the lamp.*)

JACK: We don't need that. The moon's out.

LULU: (*Puts the lamp back.*) As you wish. (*Falls round his neck.*) I wouldn't do anything to hurt you! I want you so much! Don't leave me begging any longer!

JACK: Fine by me.

(*Follows her into SCHIGOLCH's cubby-hole. The lamp goes out. On the floor between the two windows we see two four-sided patches of grey moonlight. Everything in the room can be seen.*)

GESCHWITZ: (*Alone, as if in a dream.*) This is the last night I'm spending with these people. I'll go home to Germany. My mother'll send me the money. I could take a degree, fight for women's rights...

LULU: (*Barefoot and in chemise and petticoat, opens the door screaming and holds it shut from outside.*) Help, help!

GESCHWITZ: (*Rushes to the door, pulls her revolver and points it at the door, pushing LULU behind her.*) Let go!

(*JACK tears the door open from inside and, ducking low, runs the knife into GESCHWITZ, who fires one shot into the ceiling then falls, moaning. JACK grabs the revolver from her and throws himself against the main door.*)

JACK: I'll be damned if I ever saw a prettier mouth!
(*The sweat is running from his hair, his hands are bloody. He coughs from the bottom of his lungs and stares at the floor with bulging eyes. LULU, every part of her shaking, looks around wildly. Suddenly she grabs the bottle, smashes it on the table and rushes at JACK with the broken neck in her hand. JACK lifts his right leg and throws LULU on her back. Then he picks her up from the floor.*)

LULU: No, no! – Please! – Murder! – Police! – Police!

JACK: Shut up! You're not getting away again.
(*He carries her into the cubby-hole.*)

LULU: (*Inside.*) No...no...no! Oh... Oh!
(*After a while JACK comes out and puts the basin on the table.*)

JACK: That was a job and a half. (*Washing his hands.*) I'm a lucky bastard, ain't I. (*Looks around for a hand-towel.*) Haven't even got a towel, these people. What a miserable dump! (*He dries his hands on GESCHWITZ's petticoat.*) I'm not touching this monster. (*To GESCHWITZ.*) You'll have had yours soon an' all. (*Goes through the centre door.*)

GESCHWITZ: Lulu! My angel! Let me look at you once more. I'm with you. And I'll stay with you...for ever. (*Falls to her elbows.*) Oh damn it! (*Dies.*)

The End.

THE MARQUIS OF KEITH

The characters of HERMANN CASIMIR and SASHA
may be played by girls.

The play takes place in Munich in the late summer of 1899.

Characters

THE MARQUIS OF KEITH

MOLLY GRIESINGER

CONSUL CASIMIR
a business-man

HERMANN CASIMIR
his fifteen year old son

ANNA
the widowed Countess Werdenfels

ERNST SCHOLZ
formerly Count Trautenau

SARANIEFF
a painter

RASPE
detective superintendent

OSTERMEIER
a brewer

KRENZL
a builder

GRANDAUER
a restaurateur

SASHA

SIMBA

FRAU OSTERMEIER

FREIFRAU VON TOTLEBEN
a divorcee

BUTCHER'S BOY

BAKER'S WIFE

PORTER

ACT ONE

A study, its walls lined with books. Stage right in the rear wall a door to the hall, stage left the door to an ante-room. Downstage right a door into the living room. Downstage left a desk on which are lying rolls of plans. Next to it, on the wall, a telephone. Down right a sofa with a small table in front of it. A larger table somewhat upstage centre. Bookshelves full of books, musical instruments, legal documents and sheet-music. The MARQUIS OF KEITH sits at the desk, engrossed in one of the plans. A man of about twenty-seven, medium height, slim and bony. His physique would be exemplary if not for a limp in his left leg. His pronounced features show a nervousness and hardness at the same time. Piercing grey eyes, small blond moustache, his wild, short, straw-blond hair carefully parted in the middle. He is dressed with a studied modish elegance, but not a dandy. He has the rough, red hands of a clown.

MOLLY GRIESINGER enters from the living room and sets a tray on the small table in front of the sofa. An inconspicuous brunette, somewhat reserved and agitated in plain, homely dress, but with big, black, soulful eyes.

MOLLY: Here you are, dear. Cold meat, tea and a little caviar.

KEITH: (*Not moving.*) Thank you, my dear.

MOLLY: Have you heard any more about your Hall of Wonders idea?

KEITH: Can't you see I'm working?

MOLLY: You always are when I come to see you. I have to find out about your projects from your lady-friends.

KEITH: (*Turning in his seat.*) I knew a woman once who refused to listen when I talked about my plans. She'd say 'Come and tell me when you've actually done something.'

MOLLY: I suppose I just have to put up with your knowing so many different women. (*The doorbell rings.*) Dear me, who on earth can that be?
(*She goes out into the hall.*)

KEITH: (*To himself.*) Poor thing.

MOLLY: (*Returning with a card.*) There's a young man wants to speak to you. I said you were working.

KEITH: (*Having read the card.*) Perfect timing!
(*MOLLY brings in HERMANN CASIMIR, a fifteen-year-old schoolboy in extremely stylish cycling costume, and goes into the living room.*)

HERMANN: Good morning, Herr Baron.

KEITH: What have you got for me?

HERMANN: I suppose it's best if I come straight to the point. I was with Saranieff and Samrjaki last night, in the Café Luitpold. I was telling them how I badly needed a hundred marks. Saranieff said I should come to you.

KEITH: The whole of Munich seems to take me for some sort of American railway magnate!

HERMANN: Samrjaki said you always had money.

KEITH: I supported Samrjaki because he's the greatest musical genius since Wagner. But these bandits aren't proper company for a young man like you.

HERMANN: I find these 'bandits' interesting. I got to know them at an anarchists' meeting I went to.

KEITH: That must be a pleasant surprise for your father – to find you starting your life in revolutionary gatherings.

HERMANN: Why won't he let me leave Munich!

KEITH: Because you're too young for the big, wide world.

HERMANN: Well I think you learn infinitely more by really experiencing things than by fidgeting around in a school desk till you 'come of age'.

KEITH: What does your father say about me?

HERMANN: We don't talk. I'm hardly ever home.

KEITH: That's a mistake. I followed your father's financial operations from America. He simply thinks it's impossible for anyone else to be as astute as he is. That's why he's so resolutely refused to get involved in my project so far.

HERMANN: There are higher things in life than money!

KEITH: That's what they teach you at school. These things are called 'higher' because they're only possible once you have wealth. Thanks to your father making a fortune, you have the chance to devote yourself to an artistic or scholarly career. But if you try to put yourself beyond that first rule of nature, you'll be throwing your inheritance away to the first con-man who happens along.

HERMANN: If Jesus Christ had operated on that principle –

KEITH: Christianity, remember, has freed two-thirds of the world from slavery. There is no belief – be it social, philosophical or artistic – that doesn't concern itself in the end with basic goods and chattels. And please don't believe the world will ever change in that respect. You either get used to it or you get used, full stop. (*Sits at his desk.*) I'll give you the hundred marks. But come and see me some time when you don't need money. How long is it now since your mother died?

HERMANN: It'll be three years in the spring.

KEITH: (*Gives him a sealed note.*) Take this to Countess Werdenfels. Brienner Strasse, Number 23. Give her my best wishes. I don't have any cash on me just now.

HERMANN: Thank you, sir.

KEITH: (*Sees him to the door then, shutting it behind him.*) My pleasure. (*Returns to his desk and begins hunting among his plans.*) That father of his treats me like some...ratcatcher. I must set up a concert soon! Then public opinion will force him to join me... And if the worst comes to the worst, I'll just have to go it alone. (*A knock at the door.*) Come in!

(*ANNA, the widowed Countess Werdenfels comes in. She is a voluptuous, thirty-year-old beauty. White skin, turned up nose, bright eyes, luxuriant chestnut hair. KEITH approaches her.*)

KEITH: Anna, my queen! I just sent the Casimir boy to you for a small favour.

ANNA: That was Casimir's son?

KEITH: (*Briefly kissing her offered lips.*) He'll be back when he finds you're not there.

ANNA: He doesn't look much like his father.

KEITH: I think we should forget his father. I'm turning to people now whose social ambition I fully expect to transform into boundless enthusiasm.

ANNA: But everyone says Casimir is a great supporter of young singers and actresses.

KEITH: (*Devouring her with his eyes.*) Anna, the moment I see you before me, I'm a different person. – Would you like some breakfast?

ANNA: (*Sits on the sofa and eats.*) I've got a class at eleven. Madame Bianchi says I could be the leading interpreter of Wagner within the year. Exactly *how* I'm to achieve such dizzy heights my feeble woman's brain can't quite grasp.

KEITH: I can't explain it either. I simply go with the tide. When I went out into the world my greatest hope was to die a village schoolmaster in Upper Silesia.

ANNA: And how Munich lies at your feet.

KEITH: All I knew about Munich was what I'd learned in Geography. If I enjoy a less than unblemished reputation today, people should remember how far down the scale I started.

ANNA: Every night I pray God will give me some of your astonishing energy.

KEITH: Rubbish, I have no energy at all.

ANNA: It's meat and drink to you to go charging into some battle or other.

KEITH: Whatever gifts I have are due entirely to the sad fact that the bourgeois world stifles me. After all, other people are planted at a certain level in society, vegetate there for the rest of their lives – and never come into conflict with the world at all.

ANNA: Whereas you came into the world a totally formed personality!

KEITH: I came into the world a mongrel. My father had a great mind – especially for mathematics and life's minutiae. My mother was a gypsy.

ANNA: At least you can read people's secrets from their faces. I'd love to!

KEITH: It's a skill which arouses more mistrust than I can do with. But that very bourgeois reserve is what, quite unwittingly, plays into my hands. The higher I rise, the more trusting people are towards me. All I need now is to reach that level at which the cross between philosopher and horse-thief fetches its true value.

ANNA: It really is true, you know: one hears nothing in town now but talk of your Hall of Wonders.

KEITH: The Hall is nothing more than a focus for all my skills put together.

ANNA: Yesterday you said you were building it just for me.

KEITH: But not so you could spend the rest of your life dancing up on your hind legs, atoning for it to blackmailers.

ANNA: It's true I can't show a pedigree like that Rosenkron woman or von Totleben.

KEITH: And you needn't be jealous of either.

ANNA: I should hope not!

KEITH: I inherited them from my predecessor in the concert agency. As soon as my position is secure, they can go and write novels – or hawk radishes – for all I care.

ANNA: You know, I care more for the shoes I walk in than I do for your love. And d'you know why? Because you're totally ruthless. You care about nothing but your own pleasure. That's why if you left me, I'd really feel nothing but sympathy for you. But just watch out it's not you who gets left first.

KEITH: (*Caressing her.*) It's true I have a somewhat erratic life behind me, but now I'm thinking very seriously about building my own home. I've done with the past. I've come close to death too often.

ANNA: I'm pretty indestructible myself.

KEITH: If Fate didn't intend us for each other, with our extraordinary affinity of tastes, we still have one thing in common…

ANNA: Our disgustingly rude health.

KEITH: (*Sitting next to her and caressing her.*) As far as I'm concerned, brains, beauty, good health and sensuality in a woman are all one. If she's got one, she's got the lot. And if our children fulfil their potential inheritance – (*SASHA, a thirteen-year-old errand boy in braided jacket and knee-breeches, enters from the hall and lays an armful of newspapers on the central table.*)

KEITH: Any word from Herr Ostermeier at the Chamber of Commerce?

SASHA: He gave me a letter. It's with the papers. (*Goes into the ante-room.*)

KEITH: (*Opening the letter.*) A good thing you're here. (*Reads.*) '...heard from various quarters about your plans and am keenly interested. I shall be at the Café Maximilian from midday today...' – The world's in my hands! If Casimir wants in now, he'll have to come crawling on hands and knees. What's more, with these city fathers involved, I keep personal control.

ANNA: (*Rising.*) Can you give me a thousand marks?

KEITH: Are you broke again?

ANNA: The rent's due.

KEITH: That can wait. Don't worry about it.

ANNA: If you say so. The Count warned me on his death-bed I'd be seeing the seamy side of life again before long.

KEITH: I'll send you the money in the morning.

ANNA: (*As she's escorted out.*) No, don't. I'll come and get it myself.

(*The stage remains empty for a moment, then MOLLY GRIESINGER comes in from the living room and clears the small table. Keith returns from the hall.*)

KEITH: (*Calls.*) Sasha!

(*Takes one of the pictures from the wall.*)

MOLLY: D'you really still believe we can get by that way?

SASHA: (*Entering from the ante-room.*) Herr Baron?

KEITH: (*Gives him the picture.*) Take this Saranieff over to Tannhauser. Tell him to put it in his window. I'll sell it for three thousand marks.

SASHA: Very good, sir.

KEITH: I'll be there myself in five minutes. Wait! (*He takes a card from his desk with '3000 M.' on it and fastens it in the picture-frame, then sits at his desk.*) I'll have to write an article about it first.

(*SASHA goes off with the picture.*)

MOLLY: If only there was a grain of real success in all this swaggering.

KEITH: (*Writing.*) 'Ideal Beauty in the Modern Landscape...'

MOLLY: If this Saranieff could really paint, you wouldn't need to write an article about him.

KEITH: (*Turning.*) I beg your pardon?

MOLLY: Don't tell me – you're working.

KEITH: You wanted me for something?

MOLLY: I've had a letter from Buckeburg.

KEITH: From your mother?

MOLLY: (*Pulls the letter from her pocket and reads.*) 'You're welcome here any time. You could have the two front rooms on the top floor, and rest a while till your affairs in Munich sort themselves out.'

KEITH: My dear, don't you realise correspondence like that undermines my credit?

MOLLY: We have nothing to eat tomorrow.

KEITH: Then we'll eat in the Hotel Continental.

MOLLY: And I won't he able to keep a thing down for fear the bailiffs are seizing our bed.

KEITH: All you think about is food! You could make life so much happier for yourself if only you looked more on the bright side. You have an unquenchable thirst for unhappiness.

MOLLY: It's you who wants to be unhappy! Other people find their work so easy, they never have to think about it. They can live for each other in a comfortable home, with nothing to mar their joy. While you, with all your talents, rush around on business like a madman, damaging your health, and no money in the house for days on end.

KEITH: You've always had more than enough to eat! It's not my fault you spend nothing on clothes. As soon as I've written this article we'll have three thousand marks. You can take a cab and buy every blessed thing you can think of, all at once.

MOLLY: You're as likely to get three thousand marks for that picture as I am to put on silk stockings for you.

KEITH: (*Rising reluctantly.*) You're a gem.

MOLLY: (*Flinging her arms round him.*) Have I hurt you, my pet? Forgive me, please! I only said what I truly, truly believe.

KEITH: Even if the money only lasts till tomorrow night, I shan't regret the sacrifice one moment.

MOLLY: (*Weeping.*) I know it was hateful of me.

KEITH: My Hall of Wonders is as good as built.

MOLLY: Then let me at least kiss your hand. I beg you, let me kiss your hand.

KEITH: As long as I can just keep my nerve another two or three days.

MOLLY: Not even that! How can you be so cruel!

KEITH: (*Takes his hands from his pockets.*) Perhaps it's time you listened to that inner voice of yours. Otherwise the realisation might come all of a sudden.

MOLLY: (*Jumps up, outraged.*) Just don't imagine I'm going to let myself be intimidated by these flirtations of yours! The bond that ties us is too great. The moment it breaks, I won't be able to keep you any more. But as long as you're in difficulty, you're mine.

KEITH: It could be your doom, Molly, to fear good fortune more than death. If my hands were untied tomorrow, you couldn't bear to stay with me a moment longer.

MOLLY: As long as you know that.

KEITH: The thing is, I'm not in difficulty!

MOLLY: Then let me work for you till your hands are free.

KEITH: (*Sits at his desk again.*) Do what you must! You know I like nothing less than a woman who works.

MOLLY: I'm not going to make a jackass of myself just for your sake. Even if I do stand over the laundry basin instead of parading half-naked at some fancy-dress ball with you, at least that way I shan't be the ruin of you. I'll never be happy forcing myself, pretending to be better than God made me, just for your sake – because it's me you love!

KEITH: That goes without saying.

MOLLY: (*Triumphant.*) Because you can't live without my love! Whether I stay with you depends entirely on whether I leave you enough love over for your other women. They can doll themselves up and sing your praises to their hearts' content. That saves me playing games. If it ever became serious – and we're a long way off that – I'd...bury myself alive.

KEITH: If only you'd try for once to enjoy the good fortune you're offered.

MOLLY: (*Tender.*) But what am I offered, my darling? Even in America it was always the same endless crisis. Everything always fell through in the last three days, because when it came to it we never had a bottle of brandy to offer. D'you remember shouting 'A dollar, a dollar, my republic for a dollar!'

KEITH: (*Jumps up, furious, and goes to the sofa.*) I came into this world a cripple. That doesn't condemn me to live like a slave. No more than the bad luck of being born a beggar need deprive me of my right to enjoy life to the full!

MOLLY: And you'll still be looking for that right when you die.

KEITH: If I die without having lived on this earth, I shall come back and haunt it.

MOLLY: Illusions of grandeur, that's your trouble.

KEITH: But I know where my duty lies! If we separated today, and you were left to your own devices, I hate to think how you'd end up.

MOLLY: (*Flings her arms round his neck.*) Then come back to Buckeburg! My parents haven't seen me for three years. They'll be so pleased, they'll give you half what they own. Just think how we could live!

KEITH: In Buckeburg?

MOLLY: Every cloud has a silver lining!

KEITH: (*Freeing himself.*) I'd sooner hunt for cigarette ends round the cafés.

SASHA: (*Returns with the picture.*) Herr Tannhauser says he can't put your picture in the window. He's got a dozen pictures by Mr Saranieff already.

MOLLY: What did I tell you?

KEITH: That's all you're here for! (*Goes to the desk and tears up his writing paper.*) At least I don't have to write the damn article.

(*SASHA puts the picture on the table and goes into the anteroom.*)

MOLLY: These Saranieffs and Samrjakis aren't like us. They can make people empty their pockets just like that. You and I are too simple for this world.

KEITH: Leave me alone. Buckeburg can wait a bit longer.

MOLLY: (*As the doorbell rings, claps her hands ironically.*) I knew it! The bailiffs!

(*She hurries off to answer the door.*)

KEITH: (*Looking at the time.*) What else can happen?

MOLLY: (*Leads ERNST SCHOLZ in.*) The gentleman won't give his name.

(*SCHOLZ is slim and extremely aristocratic-looking, about twenty-seven years old, black curly hair, pointed beard, large limpid blue eyes with a somewhat helpless air beneath heavy brows.*)

KEITH: Gaston! – Where've you sprung from? You look all in.

SCHOLZ: That's why I've come here. I'm in Munich only to see you.

KEITH: I'm flattered. You know, whatever time I can spare from business is yours.

SCHOLZ: I know things are a struggle for you just now. But the way you can help me is quite simple. Your personal contacts. I'd like you to offer me guidance, but on one condition: that you allow me to help you out financially – as far as you're able.

KEITH: But why? – It must be four years since we saw each other last.

SCHOLZ: The ball at the Palais de Justice in Brussels.

KEITH: You fell for the Danish Ambassador's daughter and were enraged when I suggested women were more materialistic than men could ever be.

SCHOLZ: Through our entire youth together you were to me, as you are today, the very model of unscrupulousness. But you were right.

KEITH: I don't think anyone's ever paid me a more flattering compliment.

SCHOLZ: Although I abhor everything you stand for, I'm confiding in you today the most insoluble puzzle of my life.

KEITH: Well thank God you're finally looking on the bright side!

SCHOLZ: You mustn't think this is some callow capitulation. I've tried every means I know to solve my dilemma myself – and all in vain.

KEITH: Then I'm glad that's behind you. For your sake. After all, one can throw away nothing greater than one's own life. – Weren't you going to devote yourself to public service in Brussels?

SCHOLZ: I went into the Ministry of Railways.

KEITH: I remember being surprised, with your kind of money, you didn't choose to live like a lord, taking each day as it comes.

SCHOLZ: I'd made up my mind, above all else, to be a useful member of society. Had I been born the son of a wage-earner, no doubt this would have been a matter of course.

KEITH: You can never serve your fellow man better than by pursuing your own ends as comprehensively as possible. Anyone who imagines he's making a contribution by holding down his job and feeding his children, is kidding himself. Children would thank God for not being brought into this world, and meanwhile there are a hundred poor devils breaking their necks to get their hands on your job!

SCHOLZ: But given that I am, in fact, rich, I could see no compelling reason to loaf around all day. I have no artistic inclination, yet I didn't feel insignificant enough to see my life's purpose as simply marrying and raising children.

KEITH: But you've left the Civil Service?

SCHOLZ: (*His head drops.*) I was responsible for causing a terrible accident. Now – out of nothing but a sense of duty, almost as a form of punishment – I wish to seek out pure sensual pleasure.

KEITH: What was this accident? Tell me.

SCHOLZ: I changed one of the railway regulations. There was always the danger that this particular rule could never be observed closely enough. The very first day after it was introduced a crash occurred between two express trains, killing nine men, three women and two children. I even inspected the site of the accident. It's not my fault I survived the sight of it.

KEITH: And that's when you decided to travel?

SCHOLZ: I went to England, Italy...but only now do I feel truly excluded from human activity. Even in the rowdiest company, with ear-splitting music, I'd suddenly be reminded of the accident and let out a terrible scream. Even in the Orient I lived like a frightened mouse. To put it bluntly, I'm convinced that ever since that dreadful day my only chance to win back any joy in my life is by abandoning myself entirely. But for that I need access to life. A year ago I hoped to find the way by proposing marriage to the first girl I came across from a humble background.

KEITH: You really wanted to make her the Countess Trautenau?

SCHOLZ: I'm no longer a Count. The press made great play of the contrast between my title and the horror I'd caused. I've been plain Ernst Scholz for two years now. So my engagement caused no great stir. But misfortune occurred, even from that. Not even a spark of love in her heart, and only the need for sacrifice in mine. I made a settlement on her. She's now a highly eligible party amongst her own kind. And now at last I must learn the difficult art of forgetting myself.

KEITH: (*Throws himself in an armchair.*) My father would turn in his grave at the thought of your seeking my advice.

SCHOLZ: Your father contributed mightily to my one-sided education.

KEITH: You were his model pupil. I was his whipping-boy.

SCHOLZ: But have you forgotten how tenderly the maids at our castle would kiss you? Preferably when I happened to be standing right next to you. (*Rising.*) I shall spend the next two years learning solely (*He weeps.*) how to enjoy life.

KEITH: (*Jumping up.*) We'll start tonight by going to the Nymphenburg dance-hall. It's completely beneath us, but with all the troubles raining down on me at present, I even fancy a mud-bath myself.

SCHOLZ: I have no desire to hear shrieking voices.

KEITH: I guarantee you'll forget yourself completely. In three months' time you'll look back on tonight and won't recognise yourself.

SCHOLZ: I've often wondered whether the only real source of my misfortune is indeed my monstrous wealth.

KEITH: (*Outraged.*) That is sacrilege!

SCHOLZ: If I'd had to fight for my living, I could stand on my dignity and diligence. Instead of being an outcast, I could be enjoying the most glittering career.

KEITH: Or you'd be slopping around, in love with your lowclass tart, licking the world's boots.

SCHOLZ: I'd swop that happily any day for my present fate.

KEITH: Don't pretend to yourself that railway accident stands between you and life. The only reason you're feeding on those terrible memories is because you're too cackhanded to find yourself more delicate nourishment.

SCHOLZ: You may be right at that.

KEITH: I'll find you something to get your teeth into. – I can't ask you to stay for breakfast, I'm afraid. I have a business meeting at twelve with one of our local financial bigwigs. But I'll give you a note for my friend

Raspe. Spend the afternoon with him, then we'll meet at six in the Hofgarten-Café.

(*He writes a note at his desk.*)

SCHOLZ: What is your business these days?

KEITH: I'm an art dealer, journalist, concert promoter – none of it worth a fig. But you've turned up just in time to witness the birth of an enormous concert hall, built exclusively for my artists.

SCHOLZ: (*Taking the picture from the table and examining it.*) You've got a fine collection.

KEITH: (*Getting up.*) I wouldn't sell that for ten thousand marks. A Saranieff. (*Turns it round in his hands.*) You hold it that way.

SCHOLZ: I'm completely ignorant about art. In all my travels I never visited a single museum.

KEITH: (*Gives him the note.*) This man works for the international police. So don't be too open with him. A charming man. But these people never know whether they should be keeping an eye on me, or whether I'm here to keep an eye on them.

SCHOLZ: Thank you for receiving me so kindly. Till tonight then. Six in the Hofgarten-Café.

KEITH: We'll go on to Nymphenburg. I'm glad even you have finally learnt to trust me.

(*He accompanies SCHOLZ out. The stage is empty for a moment, then MOLLY comes back and clears away the tray. KEITH comes back immediately after.*)

KEITH: Sasha! (*Goes to the telephone and rings.*) Seventeen thirty-five. – Commissioner Raspe.

SASHA: Sir?

KEITH: My hat and coat.

(*SASHA runs into the hall.*)

MOLLY: I beg you, please don't get mixed up with this chap. He wouldn't come to us if he wasn't out to exploit us.

KEITH: (*Into the phone.*) Thank Heaven you're there. Can you wait ten minutes? You'll soon find out. (*To MOLLY, as SASHA helps him into his coat.*) I'm popping over to the paper.

MOLLY: What shall I tell Mama?

KEITH: (*To SASHA.*) A cab.

SASHA: Coming up, sir.

(*He goes.*)

KEITH: Give her my respects. (*Goes to his desk.*) Plans...
Ostermeier's letter...by tomorrow morning all Munich
will know my Hall of Wonders is under way!

MOLLY: So you won't come to Buckeburg?

KEITH: (*Picking up his rolls of plans and his hat, and jams it
on.*) I wonder how on earth a man like that turns himself
into a bon viveur?

(*Hurries off.*)

End of Act One

ACT TWO

The Marquis of Keith's study. The centre table is now laid for breakfast: champagne and a huge bowl of oysters. KEITH sits on his desk with his foot on a stool while SASHA, kneeling before him, ties his boots with a buttonhook. SCHOLZ stands behind the sofa, tinkering with a guitar, which he's taken from the wall.

KEITH: What time'd you get back to your hotel this morning?

SCHOLZ: (*With a radiant smile.*) Ten.

KEITH: Was I right to leave you with that charming creature?

SCHOLZ: After all the talk we had about art and literature, I'm wondering if I shouldn't go back to school. Even more amazing, she asks to be a waitress at this garden-party you're planning.

KEITH: It's quite simple – she considers it an honour. And, incidentally, the garden-party will have to wait. I'm going to Paris for a few days.

SCHOLZ: That's awkward.

KEITH: Come with me. I want one of my artistes to sing to the Marquesi before she appears in public here.

SCHOLZ: You expect me to revive the torment I went through the last time I was there?

KEITH: Then Saranieff the painter can keep you company while I'm away. We're bound to bump into him somewhere today.

SCHOLZ: How can such a girl think it an honour to serve as your waitress?

KEITH: Because it'll give her the chance to pay back the boundless contempt in which she's held by polite society.

SCHOLZ: How can they do that? Even at her giddiest, that girl would never be guilty of a sin like the soul-destroying strife which kept my parents together twenty years.

KEITH: Tell me what sin is.

SCHOLZ: I realised fully for the first time last night: ruined lives watching on in bitter envy.

KEITH: Sin is a myth, a term people use for bad business. You can only do 'good business' inside the established order. I should know. For all my reputation across Europe, I remain as much an outcast from society as that girl. And that's the only reason I'm giving this party.

SASHA: (*Rising.*) D'you need a cab, sir?

KEITH: I do. (*SASHA goes. KEITH stamps his boots on.*) Did you see my Hall of Wonders company has been floated?

SCHOLZ: Needless to say I haven't even touched a paper since yesterday.

(*They take their places at the breakfast table.*)

KEITH: The whole operation depends on a brewer, a builder and a restaurateur. They are the caryatids supporting the pediment of my temple.

SCHOLZ: I found your friend Raspe quite delightful.

KEITH: He's a rogue. But I like him for other reasons.

SCHOLZ: He said he used to be a theology student, but lost his faith through reading too much.

KEITH: He sank lower and lower until the State finally took him to its bosom and gave him back his faith – after two years behind bars. Let me warn you again – you mustn't be too open. The truth is our most costly possession. One can't be too sparing with it.

SCHOLZ: I suppose that's why you took the name von Keith?

KEITH: I have the same right to my name as you have to yours. I'm the adopted son of Lord Keith who, in 1863 –

SASHA: (*Entering from the hall and announcing.*) Professor Saranieff.

(*SARANIEFF enters in black frock-coat – its sleeves slightly too long and bright trousers – slightly too short; rough shoes, bright red gloves, longish, spiky black hair cut straight; a Murillo-style pince-nez on a black cord in front of eyes full of portent; an expensive profile, small Spanish moustache. He gives his top hat to SASHA, after a nod of greeting.*)

SARANIEFF: My heartfelt best wishes, dear friend. At last the hawsers are cut, and the balloon can fly!

KEITH: My partners await, I'm afraid. Otherwise I'd ask you to breakfast.

SARANIEFF: (*Sitting at the table.*) I'll save you the invite.

KEITH: Sasha – another place!

(*SASHA has hung the hat up in the hall and goes into the living room.*)

SARANIEFF: My only wonder is that the great Casimir's name doesn't appear among the partners in your consortium.

KEITH: The only reason is that I wish to remain master of my own creation. (*He introduces them.*) Graf Trautenau – Herr Kunstmaler Saranieff.

SARANIEFF: (*Taking a glass and plate and serving himself.*) I already know the Count inside-out. (*To KEITH.*) Simba was just at my place. She's sitting for a Boecklin for me.

KEITH: (*Explaining, to SCHOLZ.*) Boecklin was a great painter himself. (*To SARANIEFF.*) You don't need to show off all your little tricks, you know.

SARANIEFF: Make me famous and I won't need my little tricks. I'll pay you thirty percent for life. Samrjaki's brain is already addled like some rotting gatepost because he's set on becoming immortal the honest way.

SCHOLZ: To seek immortality, I imagine one must love life to the full.

SARANIEFF: That reminds me. Our Simba described you as a highly interesting man.

SCHOLZ: I can well believe that miserable devils like me don't come her way every day.

SARANIEFF: She decided you belonged to the Symbolists. (*To KEITH.*) And then she got very enthusiastic about a forthcoming fireworks party to launch your Hall of Wonders.

KEITH: You don't fool anyone with fireworks, but even the most rational being feels slighted if you don't offer him a show.

SARANIEFF: (*To SCHOLZ.*) I understand a washerwoman at the foot of the pyramids changed your shirt-collar?

SCHOLZ: You really do seem to be terribly well informed about me. Perhaps I could visit your studio some time.

SARANIEFF: If you like, we could take our coffee there. Simba will still be there.

SCHOLZ: Simba? You keep talking about Simba. The girl told me her name was Kathi.

SARANIEFF: Her real name's Kathi, but the Marquis christened her Simba.

SCHOLZ: A reference to that wonderful mane of red hair, no doubt.

KEITH: That's a subject I choose not to enlarge upon.

(*MOLLY comes from the living room and lays a place for SARANIEFF.*)

SARANIEFF: My deepest gratitude, good lady. As you can see I've already eaten my fill. Forgive me for not kissing your hand before.

MOLLY: Spare your compliments for a more deserving opportunity.

(*The doorbell off. MOLLY goes to answer. KEITH looks at his watch and gets up.*)

KEITH: You'll have to excuse me, gentlemen. – Sasha!

SARANIEFF: (*Wiping his mouth.*) No problem, we'll come with you.

(*He and SCHOLZ rise. SASHA enters from the ante-room with their coats and helps KEITH and SCHOLZ into their overcoats.*)

SCHOLZ: (*To KEITH.*) Why didn't you tell me you were married?

KEITH: Let me straighten your cravat. (*Does it.*) You should take more care of your appearance.

(*MOLLY comes back from the hall with HERMANN CASIMIR.*)

MOLLY: Young Herr Casimir asks if he can see you.

KEITH: (*To HERMANN.*) Did you pass on my greetings yesterday?

HERMANN: The Countess was hoping for money from *you*!

KEITH: Wait for me here a moment. I'll be straight back. (*To SCHOLZ and SARANIEFF.*) Are we ready, gentlemen?

SARANIEFF: (*Taking his hat from SASHA.*) To hell and back!

SASHA: The cab's waiting, sir.

KEITH: You sit with the coachman.

(*The four leave.*)

MOLLY: I can't think what you want in this madhouse. You'd really be far better off safe at home with your Mama.

HERMANN: (*Thinking he should go immediately.*) My mother's dead, Madam, but I don't want to be a nuisance.

MOLLY: For goodness sake, stay. You're not disturbing me. I just wonder about the kind of parents who expose their children to robbers like these. I had a happy home like you when I was your age. And I too leapt into the unknown without a moment's thought.

HERMANN: But I'll die if I stay in Munich any longer. – You mustn't tell the Marquis, though. He wouldn't help me if he knew my plans.

MOLLY: Just so long as you don't end up worse off than me. If only my mother had made me work as I do now, instead of sending me skating on my afternoons off, I'd still have a life to look forward to today.

HERMANN: But if you're so unhappy and know…well, that you could be happy again, why don't you…just get divorced?

MOLLY: To get a divorce, you have to he married first.

HERMANN: I'm sorry. I thought…I mean, I thought you were married.

MOLLY: To be married, you need papers. And getting papers is beneath his dignity. (*The doorbell rings.*) It's like the post office in this house. Open all hours! (*Goes out to the hall.*)

HERMANN: (*Pulling himself together.*) How could I be such a blabber-mouth?

MOLLY: (*Leading ANNA in.*) If you don't mind waiting for my husband here. He should be back soon. May I introduce you?

ANNA: Thank you, we've already met.

MOLLY: Naturally! Then you don't need me, do you.
(*Off into the living-room.*)

ANNA: (*Lowering herself on to the desk chair and laying her hand on HERMANN's.*) Now tell me frankly, young man, exactly why d'you need so much money while you're still at school?

HERMANN: I'm not telling.

ANNA: I'd really like to know.

HERMANN: I bet you would.

ANNA: Spoilsport.

HERMANN: (*Removing his hand.*) I won't be treated like this.

ANNA: Treated like what? You're imagining things. – Look, I'll tell you something. I always divide people into two categories. Some are lickety-split, the rest are mimsypimsy.

HERMANN: In your eyes of course I'm mimsy-pimsy.

ANNA: If you can't even say why you need so much money…

HERMANN: Not because I'm mimsy-pimsy, that's for sure!

ANNA: I knew from the moment I saw you – you're licketysplit!

HERMANN: That's right. Otherwise I'd be happy enough to stay in Munich.

ANNA: So you want to get out in the world.

HERMANN: And you'd like to know where. Well then: Paris, London –

ANNA: Paris isn't 'in' any more.

HERMANN: Who said I want to go to Paris.

ANNA: Why not stay here in Munich? You've got a filthy rich father –

HERMANN: Nothing ever happens here! A friend who used to be in my class at school wrote to me from Africa. He said, if you feel miserable in Africa you still feel ten times better than when you feel happy in Munich.

ANNA: I'll tell you something. Your friend is mimsy. Don't go to Africa. Stay here with us and enjoy life.

HERMANN: But you can't here!

(*MOLLY leads in Commissioner RASPE. RASPE, in his early twenties, in light summer suit and boater, has the harmless, childlike look of an angel by Guido Reni. Short blond hair, beginnings of a moustache. When he feels himself watched, he jams a pince-nez on.*)

MOLLY: My husband'll be back any moment, if you don't mind waiting. May I introduce –

RASPE: Madam, I'm not sure it's in the Baron's best interest to introduce me.

MOLLY: In that case I won't. – Dearie me!

(*Off to the living room.*)

ANNA: I have to tell you your caution is unnecessary. We've already met.

RASPE: (*Sitting on the sofa.*) Ah. I'm afraid I'll need to think back...

ANNA: When you've finished thinking. I'd be grateful not to be introduced either.

RASPE: How come I haven't heard about you around here?

ANNA: What's in a name? I've heard about you though. Apparently you spent a couple of years in total retreat.

RASPE: I couldn't help it. I was a victim of the absurd trust everyone had in me.

ANNA: But now you're on your toes again?

RASPE: Nowadays I simply utilise the absurd trust people have in me to the benefit of my fellow-man. – D'you know anything about this would-be bon viveur, Herr Scholz?

ANNA: I'm sorry. Our paths haven't crossed.

RASPE: He's quite harmless. I hardly knew what to do with him. I began his education in the Hofbrauhaus. It's just round the corner.

(*MOLLY opens the door and ushers in CONSUL CASIMIR, a man in his mid-forties, thickset, elegantly and opulently dressed, full-faced and with luxurious black sideburns, a full moustache, bushy eyebrows and hair carefully parted in the middle.*)

MOLLY: My husband isn't home. (*Goes.*)

CASIMIR: (*Without acknowledging anyone else, goes straight to HERMANN.*) The door's that way. Of all places, I find you in this vipers' den.

HERMANN: And you wouldn't come looking for me here if you didn't fear for your investments.

CASIMIR: (*Crowding him.*) Will you be quiet! – Do I have to force you?

HERMANN: (*Pulls a small revolver.*) Don't touch me, father! Lay one finger on me and I'll shoot myself.

CASIMIR: You'll pay for this when I get you home!

ANNA: (*Stepping in front of him.*) Please sir, there'll be an accident. If you could just calm yourself... (*To HERMANN.*) Why not be sensible? Go with your father.

HERMANN: There's nothing there for me. He wouldn't even notice if I drank myself senseless.

ANNA: Then just tell him calmly what your plans are, but don't threaten him with a revolver. Give it here.

HERMANN: Why didn't I think of that!

ANNA: You won't regret it, believe me. You can have it back when you've calmed down. – D'you think I'd lie to you? (*HERMANN hesitates then gives her the revolver.*) Now ask your father's forgiveness. If you've an ounce of honour, you can't expect him to make the first move.

HERMANN: I... I...beg your... (*He falls to his knees and sobs.*)

ANNA: (*Tries to pick him up.*) Shame on you! Now come on, look him in the eye.

CASIMIR: She has his mother's nerve.

ANNA: Show your father he can put his trust in you. – Now, go home, and when you've calmed down again, tell your father all your hopes and plans.
(*She leads him off.*)

CASIMIR: (*To RASPE.*) Who is that woman?

RASPE: I haven't seen her for two years. In those days she was a shop-assistant in the Perusastrasse and her name was Huber. But if you want to know more –

CASIMIR: Thank you. I'm your servant.

(*He goes. MOLLY comes out of the living-room, to take the breakfast things out.*)

RASPE: Excuse me, Madam. Did the Marquis really plan being back before lunch?

MOLLY: Please, don't bother me with trivial questions like that!

ANNA: (*Coming back in from the hall, to MOLLY.*) Might I take something from you?

MOLLY: You ask if you might take something from me? (*Putting the tray back on the table.*) Help yourselves! Clear the table! I wasn't sitting there anyway! (*Off into the living room.*)

RASPE: You handled the boy brilliantly.

ANNA: (*Sits at the desk again.*) I wouldn't mind the carriage his father took him home in.

RASPE: Tell me, whatever happened to that Count Werdenfels – the one who was always giving champagne parties?

ANNA: I bear his name.

RASPE: I'm not surprised. Please congratulate the Count on his taste for me, will you?

ANNA: That wouldn't be possible, I'm afraid.

RASPE: Ah, you live apart?

ANNA: (*As there are voices in the corridor.*) I'll tell you some other time.

(*KEITH enters with Herr OSTERMEIER, Herr KRENZL and Herr GRANDAUER. All three are heavy-bellied, bleary-eyed, suburban bourgeois. SASHA follows them in.*)

KEITH: This has turned out perfectly! May I introduce you immediately to one of our foremost artistes... Sasha, take that out, will you please? (*SASHA goes off with the breakfast tray.*) Herr Ostermeier, brewer, Herr Krenzl, builder, and Herr Grandauer, restaurateur – the caryatids of my Hall of Wonders. – The Countess Werdenfels. However, your time is precious, gentlemen, you wish to see the plans.

(*Takes the plans from his desk and unrolls them on the centre table.*)

OSTERMEIER: Tek tha time, old chap. Five minutes 'ere or there meks no difference.

KEITH: (*To GRANDAUER.*) If you could hold this end... What you see here is the concert hall, with its false ceiling and lighting, so it can also serve as a gallery in summer. Next to it a studio theatre I'd like to make popular with the very latest genres. The most modern is always the cheapest – and the most effective – form of publicity.

OSTERMEIER: Ahuh...tha've not forgotten bogs, 'ave tha?

KEITH: Here you can see how we've provided wardrobe and toiler faciliries in the most radical manner. – Here, Herr Krenzl, the front elevation – steps up, tympanum, caryatids.

KRENZL: Are they supposed to be us?

KEITH: That's just a little joke of mine, gentlemen.

GRANDAUER: Main thing for me, tha knows, as a restaurateur wi' this kind a malarkey, is space. Bags on it.

KEITH: The entire ground floor is projected as a refreshment area, Herr Grandauer.

GRANDAUER: Folk won't put up wi' bein' cooped up when they're eatin' like they would fer a show, tha knows.

KEITH: For afternoon coffee, Herr Grandauer, we have here a terrace on the first floor with the most marvellous views.

OSTERMEIER: Well the only thing outstanding, my dear chap, is a look at your flotation budget.

KEITH: (*Producing papers.*) Four thousand shares at five thousand each adds up to a round twenty million. I'm working on the assumption that each of us will sign up for forty preferred shares and buy in immediately. The projected profit, as you can see, is set unusually low.

KRENZL: We still need to know if Council'll go along wi' it.

KEITH: That's why we're issuing, alongside shares, a number of rights certificates, placed at the City's disposal – for welfare purposes, naturally. We're counting on Board members receiving ten percent of net profit after deductions for discounts and capital reserves.

OSTERMEIER: Can't say fairer'n that.

KEITH: We'll need to work the market a little, of course. Which is why I'm travelling to Paris tomorrow. A fortnight today we'll have our founding celebration at my villa in the Brienner Strasse.
(*ANNA twitches.*)

OSTERMEIER: Better invite Consul Casimir to your celebration, get 'im in on it.

KRENZL: Aye, makes sense. Wi' Casimir on our side, it'll go through Council on t' nod.

KEITH: I'm hoping to call a General Meeting before our party, gentlemen, and we'll see then if I still need to heed your proviso in respect of Consul Casimir.

OSTERMEIER: (*Shaking his hand.*) In that case I'll just say 'bong voyarge', old pal. (*Bows to ANNA.*) My compliments, madame.

GRANDAUER: And mine.

KRENZL: Cheers.
(*KEITH accompanies them out. When he returns.*)

ANNA: What on earth are you thinking of, holding your launch party in my house?

KEITH: I'll have such a costume made in Paris for you to sing in, you won't even need a voice. (*To RASPE.*) And I'm expecting you, Commissioner, to bring the full charm of your personality to bear on my caryatids' wives.

RASPE: They'll have no cause for complaint.

KEITH: (*Giving him money.*) Here's three hundred marks. I'll be bringing fireworks back from Paris the like of which Munich has never seen.

RASPE: (*Pocketing the money.*) He got this from his bon viveur.

KEITH: (*To ANNA.*) I value every mortal soul according to his ability, but to my closer acquaintances I'd command a certain caution in their dealings with Commissioner Raspe.

RASPE: Living honestly with a face looks like it's carved from a gallows like yours is nothing. I'd like to see how far you'd get with a baby face like mine!

KEITH: With your face I'd have married a princess.

ANNA: (*To RASPE.*) If I remember right, you had a French name when I first got to know you.

RASPE: Not any more. I've become a useful member of society since then. I'll be off then – if that's all right. (*Goes.*)

ANNA: My servants aren't used to giving big dinners!

KEITH: (*Calls.*) Sasha!

SASHA: (*Coming from the ante-room.*) Sir?

KEITH: Would you like to help out at the garden party at my friend's?

SASHA: Love to, sir. (*Off.*)

KEITH: Now, perhaps you'll let me introduce you to my oldest school-friend, Count Trautenau?

ANNA: I don't seem to have much luck with Counts.

KEITH: No matter. All I ask is that you don't go into my domestic arrangements with him. He's a confirmed moraliser, both by nature and conviction.

ANNA: Good heavens, he's nor the one trying to turn himself into a bon viveur, is he?

KEITH: Ironic, isn't it. All the time I've known him he's lived in a state of permanent self-sacrifice but never known he's got – ach! – two souls *in seiner Brust.*

ANNA: That too, eh, I find one quite hard enough. – But I thought his name was Scholz.

KEITH: One soul's called Scholz, the other's Graf Trautenau.

ANNA: Then thank you, no. I won't have anything to do with people who can't sort themselves out!

KEITH: Why are you getting so excited about it?

ANNA: You're trying to team me up with a monster.

KEITH: He's as quiet as a lamb.

ANNA: No thanks! I'm not letting misfortune personified into *my* boudoir.

KEITH: You misunderstand me. I need his trust right now. If he doesn't get to know you, so much the better. I won't need to fear his reproaches.

ANNA: I thought you wanted me to whore for you.

KEITH: (*Embracing her.*) Anna! I'm going to Paris tomorrow
not to work the marker or buy fireworks but because I
need fresh air – because I need to stretch my limbs if
I'm not to lose my upper hand here in Munich. Would I
take you with me if you didn't mean everything to me?
ANNA: To Paris then!
(*They embrace.*)

End of Act Two

ACT THREE

A room, lit with electric lamps, leading through a wide, glass door, right, into a garden. The middle door in the rear wall leads into the dining room, where people are eating. When the door is open, the end of the banquet-table is visible. A curtained door left to a gaming room, which also gives access to the dining-room. Near this, a small piano. Down right a lady's writing desk, down left a two-seater sofa, armchairs, small table, etc. Upstage right in the corner a door leads to the hall. A toast is being proposed in the dining room. As the glasses clink, KEITH, in evening dress, comes into the room. He holds a telegram and reads.

KEITH: 'The founding of the Munich Hall of Wonders Company yesterday brought together the cream of that happy town on the Isar to an extremely lively garden party at the Marquis of Keith's villa in the Brienner Strasse. A magnificent firework display delighted inhabitants of nearby streets till midnight. May we wish this enterprise, begun so auspiciously...' Now, who can I get to take this to the telegraph office for me? (*SCHOLZ enters from the hall, in evening dress and overcoat.*) You took your time.

SCHOLZ: I've only come to say I can't stay.

KEITH: And make me look stupid? Old Casimir's let me down as it is. But at least he sent a good luck telegram.

SCHOLZ: I don't belong here! You say you stand outside society. I stand outside humanity.

KEITH: But haven't you been enjoying everything anyone could dream of?

SCHOLZ: Enjoying what? The flood of pleasures I've been wallowing in would leave nothing to distinguish between me and...a barrow boy. Misfortune, which used to arouse my sympathy I now find almost unbearably unattractive. All this, and I'm still no nearer my goal!
(*Goes to leave.*)

KEITH: (*Holding him back.*) Any fool can have bad luck. The art is to make the most of it.

SCHOLZ: I can't stay here. Yesterday I met Countess Werdenfels. I don't know what I did to offend her. Perhaps without realising, I fell into a tone I've got used to from being with our Simba.

KEITH: Listen, I've been slapped by more women than I've got hairs on my head.

SCHOLZ: I'm totally ill-bred! And that with a woman for whom I have the most enormous respect. – And then there's young Simba herself, playing the waitress here tonight. A situation even the most skilful diplomat would find testing.

KEITH: Simba won't know you!

SCHOLZ: I'm not afraid of her being too familiar. I'm afraid of offending her by ignoring her for no good reason.

KEITH: Simba knows her way around the social graces a hundred times better than you do.

SCHOLZ: And they are precisely the bonds in which mankind discovers most vividly just how impotent he is!

KEITH: Come on, the best thing for you is to leave that coat next door!

SCHOLZ: Please forgive me! I can't possibly speak calmly to the Countess tonight.

KEITH: Then stick to the two divorcees. They're struggling with a similar problem to yours.

SCHOLZ: Two at once?

KEITH: Neither of them a day over twenty-five, perfect beauties, old Nordic aristocracy, but so modern in their outlook they make me feel like a flintlock musket.

SCHOLZ: Modern women, that's all I need!
    (*He goes off into the gaming room. KEITH is about to follow when SARANIEFF enters from the hall.*)

SARANIEFF: Is there any food left?

KEITH: Leave your coat outside please! – I haven't eaten all day myself.

SARANIEFF: They won't stand on ceremony here, will they. But I need to talk to you first about something very important.

132

(*Hangs his hat and coat up in the hall. Meanwhile SASHA enters from the gaming room in tails and satin knickerbockers with a full champagne cooler, heading for the dining room.*)

KEITH: If you're setting off the fireworks after that, Sasha, watch out for that mortar thing! It's got heaven knows what in.

SASHA: It don' worry me, master!

(*Off into the dining room, shutting the door.*)

SARANIEFF: (*Back from the hall.*) Got any money?

KEITH: You've only just sold a picture! Why d'you think I sent you my old school pal?

SARANIEFF: Only after you'd squeezed him dry yourself. He's got to wait three days before he can give me a penny.

KEITH: (*Gives him a note.*) There. A thousand.

(*SIMBA, a real Bavarian belle, fresh-cheeked, with rich red hair in a tasteful black dress with a white pinafore, enters with a light step from the dining room, carrying a tray full of half-empty wine glasses.*)

SIMBA: Th' chap from t' Chamber of Commerce wants to make you another toast.

(*KEITH takes one of her glasses and steps through the open door to the end of the table. SIMBA goes off into the games room.*)

KEITH: Ladies and gentlemen! Tonight's celebration marks the beginning of an era for Munich – one which will overshadow all that has gone before. We are creating a haven for the arts in which every art form known to man will find its spiritual home. I raise my glass to honour those elements of our life here in Munich who have ordained our city a cultural monument – to the burghers of Munich and their beautiful wives!

(*As the glasses clink, SASHA comes out of the dining room, shuts the door behind him and goes off into the gaming room. SIMBA comes out of the gaming room with a huge bell-shaped cheese, and heads for the dining room.*)

SARANIEFF: (*Stopping her.*) Simba! Have you been struck blind or what? Haven't you noticed? Any moment now

your bon viveur is going to fall into the clutches of our
Countess from the Perusastrasse.

SIMBA: What are tha doing out 'ere? Go on wi' yer, join t'
others at table.

SARANIEFF: Me, sit with the caryatids? Simba! D'you
want to see all that lovely money in your bon viveur's
pocket go to waste on this crazy Marquis?

SIMBA: Come on, let me by. I'm supposed to be servin'!

SARANIEFF: The caryatids don't need any more cheese.
(*Puts the cheese-plate on the table and takes her on his knee.*)
Simba, don't I mean anything to you any more? Are you
going to leave me begging and screaming for twenty-
mark bits from the Marquis, my teeth chattering, while
you pull thousand mark notes like rabbits out of a hat?

SIMBA: Thanks very much! I've had more bother from that
bon viveur an' 'is daft sympathy than anyone. Tries to
tell me I'm a martyr to civilisation. I told him, you
ought to tell your society ladies that, cos they're
certainly nowt else. Me, when I've drunk a bottle of
champagne an' enjoyed mesen to the full, that's when I'm
a martyr to civilisation – th' next mornin'! He asks me,
why is he a man? Do I go round axin' folk why I'm a
lass? Just one time I've seen 'im laugh. I told 'im he had
to learn cyclin'. So we go bikin' to Schleissheim, an' as
we get to the woods, a storm breaks out like it's the end
of the world. An' there, for the first time since I've
known 'im, he starts laughin'. Well, I said, you're enjoyin'
yersen now all right. The more it thundered an'
lightninged, the madder 'e laughs. Don't go under that
tree, I says, th' lightnin'll only bring it down. The
lightning won't get me, 'e says an' laughs an' laughs.

SARANIEFF: Simba, Simba, you should've been born an
aristo!

SIMBA: Thanks a lot! A social democrat is what I coulda
been. Mekkin' t' world a better place, mekkin' folk
happy, that's their speciality. But I can't really go fer t'
social democrats. Once they got into power, there'd be
no more champagne suppers.

(*RASPE, dressed in the most elegant evening suit with a small chain and medals on his breast, comes out of the games room.*)

RASPE: Simba, have you no shame? Keeping the entire Hall of Wonders party waiting for its cheese!

SIMBA: (*Grabbing the cheese.*) Jesus'n'Mary, I'm off!

SARANIEFF: And *you* ought to stick to the old bags you're being paid to keep happy.

SIMBA: (*Taking RASPE's arm.*) You leave this young lad alone. You'd he glad enough if you were built as nice as he is.

SARANIEFF: Simba, you were born a whore!

SIMBA: Wrong, I weren't born a whore. I were born a cheese-parer.

(*She goes off with RASPE into the gaming room. SASHA comes from the games room with a lit lantern.*)

SARANIEFF: God, you're tarted up! Don't tell me, you're looking for a Countess to marry as well?

SASHA: I'm goin' to light fireworks in t' garden. Watch out for the big mortar. The Marquis says all hell'll be let loose.

(*He goes into the garden as the guests pour into the room, RASPE first, leading FRAU OSTERMEIER and Freifrau von TOTLEBEN, then KEITH with OSTERMEIER, KRENZL and GRANDAUER, and lastly SCHOLZ and ANNA. SARANIEFF takes his place at the table in the dining room.*)

RASPE: May I offer the ladies a cup of finest mokka?

FRAU OSTERMEIER: I must say, a more gracious gentleman you won't find in the whole of South Germany!

TOTLEBEN: Our aristocratic equerries could take a leaf or two out of your book!

RASPE: Every moment, I swear, this is the most blessed time of my life.

OSTERMEIER: (*To KEITH.*) I must say it's nice of old Casimir to send a good luck telegram. Cos, you know, he's a damn careful man, that Casimir.

KEITH: No matter, no matter! Casimir will be one of us by
our first General Meeting. – Can I interest you
gentlemen in some coffee?

TOTLEBEN: Now then, Marquis, you must promise me
you'll teach me to become a dancer for your Hall of
Wonders.

KEITH: I swear to you, my goddess, we couldn't open it
without you.

TOTLEBEN: Oh I say! All those lights! – Come sir,
accompany us into the garden.

KEITH: (*Following other guests into the garden.*) For heaven's
sake keep well clear of that mortar. It's got all the
biggest rockets in it!
(*Everyone goes into the garden, while SIMBA closes the door
from the dining-room from the inside. ANNA and SCHOLZ
remain alone.*)

ANNA: I can't think what I'm supposed to have taken
offence at. Are you sure it wasn't some other lady you
were tactless with?

SCHOLZ: There's no chance of that. For you see, I'm as
happy as someone who's spent his life in a dungeon and
now suddenly breathes free air for the first time. I
tremble at my good fortune. If I could succeed in putting
my life at the service of some genuine good cause, I
could never thank my Creator enough.

ANNA: I thought you were in Munich to live it up.

SCHOLZ: That's just a means to an end. I give you my
solemn word. Please, you mustn't think me a hypocrite.
The thicker the blows fall, the more precious this flesh
becomes to me, flesh which till now has been an
unspeakable burden. And there's one thing I'm quite sure
of: whether my path is up or down, I shall only be
obeying the terrible, merciless instinct for self-
preservation.

ANNA: Perhaps the only reason famous people become
famous is because consorting with the rest of us *hoi polloi*
just gets on their nerves.

SCHOLZ: You still misunderstand me, Countess. The
moment I've found my niche, I shall be the humblest,

most grateful citizen. I've already taken up bicycling here in Munich. It was as if I'd never really noticed the world since my childhood. Every tree, every river, the hills, the sky – like some great revelation I'd glimpsed in another existence. – Might I invite you to a bicycling trip some time?

ANNA: Would tomorrow at seven suit you? Or perhaps you don't like to rise too early?

SCHOLZ: Tomorrow morning at seven! I see my life spread before me like an endless landscape in spring!

ANNA: But don't keep me waiting!

(*Freifrau von TOTLEBEN and FRAU OSTERMEIER come back from the garden. SIMBA comes in from the games room.*)

TOTLEBEN: Brr, it's cold out there. We'll have to take our shawls later, Martha. Play a can-can, Samrjaki! (*To SCHOLZ.*) Do you dance the can-can?

SCHOLZ: Sadly not, Madam.

TOTLEBEN: (*To FRAU OSTERMEIER.*) Then we'll have to dance together. (*SAMRJAKI plays a waltz.*) D'you call that a can-can, Mr Conductor?

ANNA: (*To SIMBA.*) But you dance the waltz, don't you?

SIMBA: If Her Grace insists...

ANNA: Come on then!

(*The women dance. KEITH comes back from the garden and turns all but a few lights out, so that the room is only dimly lit.*)

TOTLEBEN: Why's it gone dark all of a sudden?

KEITH: So my rockets can make a bigger impression! Ladies and gentlemen, it's my pleasure to be able to announce that in the next few weeks the first of our great Festival Concerts will take place, as publicity for our cause amongst Munich's great public. Countess Werdenfels will be representing us with several songs in the very latest style of composition, while our conductor, Herr Samrjaki, will himself conduct several extracts from his symphonic opus 'The Wisdom of the Brahmin'.

(*General applause. A rocket hisses upward in the garden, spreading a reddish glow into the room. KEITH turns the light out completely and opens the glass doors.)* Everyone in the garden, ladies and gentlemen!

(A second rocket goes up, as remaining guests leave the salon. KEITH, about to follow them, is held back by ANNA. The stage remains dark.)

ANNA: How come you're suddenly announcing my participation in this concert of yours?

KEITH: If you want to wait till your teacher declares you fit and ready, you could grow old and grey and never have sung a note. *(Throws himself into an armchair.)* At last this endless, endless tightrope walking is over. For ten years it's taken all my energy just to avoid falling off. From today it's onward and upward!

ANNA: And where am I supposed to find the impudence to appear before 'Munich's great public' with my singing?

KEITH: I thought you were about to become Germany's leading interpreter of Wagner.

ANNA: I said that as a joke.

KEITH: How was I supposed to know!

ANNA: A concert anywhere else would take months of preparation!

KEITH: I haven't gone without for so long in order to follow other people's examples. Anyone who doesn't like your singing will be bowled over by your astounding Parisian frock.

ANNA: The moment you clap eyes on me, you start having fantasies.

KEITH: *(Leaping up.)* I can hardly be accused of ever having overestimated women, but in you I recognised something from the very first moment. All right, our paths had crossed a few times before. But you were either in the possession of another bandit like me, or my circumstances were so reduced there was no point in entering your field of vision.

ANNA: Your taking leave of your senses because you love me is no reason for me to draw all Munich's ridicule upon myself.

KEITH: Other women have taken all sorts of things upon themselves on my account.

ANNA: But I haven't lost my wits over you.

KEITH: They all say that. Abandon yourself to your inevitable good fortune. I'll inspire you with the ease you'll need for your first appearance – even if I have to goad you on with a loaded revolver!

ANNA: Start treating me like livestock, and you and I are finished.

KEITH: D'you really think I'd be setting up this concert if I wasn't absolutely certain it'll bring you the most glittering triumph? – Remember this, I'm a man of belief... (*Another rocket rises, hissing, in the garden.*) ...I have no greater belief than that our endeavours and sacrifices in this world are rewarded.

ANNA: They'd have to be, to run yourself as ragged as you do.

KEITH: And if it doesn't come to us, then to our children.

ANNA: But you haven't got any!

KEITH: They'll be your gift to me, Anna. Children with my brains, aristocratic hands and bursting with health. And for that I'll build you a majestic home, as befits a woman of your standing. With a husband beside you fully equipped to fulfil every wish that emanates from those big, black eyes! (*He kisses her passionately. A firework is set off in the garden which illuminates the pair for a moment in a dark red glow.*) You go into the garden. My caryatids are just panting to kneel at the feet of our godhead!

ANNA: Aren't you coming too?

KEITH: (*Turns the lights up so the room is dimly lit.*) I've just got to write an announcement of our concert for the papers. It has to be in tomorrow. In it I congratulate you in advance on your outstanding triumph.

(*ANNA goes off into the garden. KEITH sits at the table and jots down a few words. MOLLY, a bright shawl round her head, hurries in from the hall, disturbed and excited.*)

MOLLY: I have to speak with you a moment.

KEITH: As long as you like, my dear. You're not disturbing me. I told you you wouldn't be able to stand it on your own in the house.

MOLLY: I just pray to God some disaster will befall us. It's the only thing can save us now!

KEITH: Then why won't you accompany me when I ask you?

MOLLY: (*Shuddering.*) Amongst these people?

KEITH: 'These people' are the business we live from. What you can't bear is that I should be here with my thoughts and not with you.

MOLLY: Is it any wonder? You're so good, so dear, so wonderful…but when you're with these people, to me you're…worse than dead!

KEITH: Go home and put something nice on. Sasha can go with you. You shouldn't be alone tonight.

MOLLY: Yes I'm just in the mood to doll myself up, aren't I. The way you're carrying on worries me so much. I feel as if the world could end tomorrow. As if there's something I must do, whatever it might be, to save us from disaster.

KEITH: As from yesterday I'm on an annual income of 100,000 marks a year. You need no longer fear we're going to die of hunger.

MOLLY: Don't make fun of me! What you're doing to me is sinful! I don't even dare say what I'm afraid of…

KEITH: Then just tell me what I can do to calm you. It'll be done in a trice.

MOLLY: Come with me! Leave this den of thieves. You're so stupid. – Yes, you are! You let yourself be taken in, your throat cut, by the lowest, commonest tricksters.

KEITH: My dear, it's better to suffer wrongdoing than to commit it.

MOLLY: Yes, if you were only conscious of it! But you can bet these types won't open your eyes. They flatter you into believing you're some kind of marvel of diplomacy and artfulness, because your vanity aims no higher, and all the time they're quietly and cold-bloodedly tying the noose round your neck!

KEITH: What are you afraid of that's so terrible?

MOLLY: (*Whimpering.*) I can't say it! I can't give it words..

KEITH: Please, spit it out. Then you'll laugh at it.

MOLLY: I'm afraid, I'm afraid...

(*A muffled explosion sounds from the garden. MOLLY screams and falls to her knees.*)

KEITH: (*Pulling her to her knees.*) That was the big mortar. – You must calm down! Look, drink a couple of glasses of champagne, then we'll watch the fireworks together.

MOLLY: The fireworks have been burning my insides for a fortnight! – You went to Paris! – With whom? – I swear to God, I'll forget I was ever afraid for you, ever suffered a thing, if you'll only come with me now!

KEITH: (*Kisses her.*) Poor thing.

MOLLY: A hand-out. – All right, all right, I'll go...

KEITH: Stay here! What's got into your head? – Dry your eyes. Someone's coming up from the garden.

MOLLY: (*Falls passionately around his neck and kisses him.*) My dear...my darling...my angel! (*She lets go, smiling.*) I just wanted to see you once amongst people. You know how I've been lately...

(*She presses her fist to her forehead.*)

KEITH: (*Tries to hold her back.*) You're staying here, my girl...

(*MOLLY rushes out through the hall door. SCHOLZ enters through the glass doors from the garden, limping and holding his knee.*)

SCHOLZ: (*Delighted.*) No please, don't worry. – Put the light out, so they can't see me from outside. None of your friends saw a thing.

(*He drags himself to an armchair and lowers himself into it.*)

KEITH: What on earth did you do?

SCHOLZ: Put the light out first. It's nothing really. The big mortar exploded, and a piece of it hit me in the knee.

KEITH: (*Has put the light out, the stage is in darkness.*) That could only happen to you.

SCHOLZ: (*Blissful.*) The pain's beginning to wear off. – Believe me, I'm the happiest creature on God's earth. Although I shan't be able to make the bicyling trip tomorrow morning with Countess Werdenfels. But what does that matter? (*Rejoicing.*) I've fought back the evil spirits. Happiness lies before me. I belong to life! From tonight, I'm a new man!

(*A rocket climbs up in the garden and lights up SCHOLZ's face with a dark red glow.*)

KEITH: Well I'm damned – I really wouldn't have recognised you!

SCHOLZ: (*Jumps out of his chair and hops around the room on one foot, rejoicing.*) For ten years I've considered myself an outcast. Beyond the pale. And to think it was all an illusion! All an illusion!

End of Act Three

ACT FOUR

Room leading to Countess WERDENFELS' garden. Several huge bouquets lie on chairs. An impressive bunch of flowers stands in a vase on the table. ANNA, in smart day-clothes is in conversation with Commissioner RASPE and HERMANN CASIMIR. It is morning.

ANNA: (*A piece of coloured notepaper in her hand, to HERMANN.*) You I must thank, my dear young friend, for your lovely verses about my concert, and for the wonderful flowers. (*To RASPE.*) However, I find it strange in you, sir, to bring me these questionable rumours about your friend and benefactor today of all days.

RASPE: The Marquis of Keith is neither my friend nor my benefactor. Two years ago I asked him to appear as a psychiatric expert at my trial. He could have saved me a year and a half in prison. Instead of which the rat goes off with a slip of a girl on a whirlwind tour of America.
(*SIMBA comes in from the hall in tasteful servant's costume and hands ANNA a card.*)

SIMBA: The gentleman craves your indulgence.

ANNA: (*To HERMANN.*) Dear Lord, it's your father!

HERMANN: (*Surprised, looking at RASPE.*) How could he possibly know I was here?

RASPE: Through me.

ANNA: (*Drawing the curtain to the games room.*) Go in here. I'll send him on his way.
(*HERMANN goes off into the games room.*)

RASPE: Then it's probably best I go too.

ANNA: Yes, if you don't mind.

RASPE: (*Bows.*) Madam.
(*Goes.*)

ANNA: (*To SIMBA.*) Ask the gentleman to come in, will you?
(*SIMBA leads in CONSUL CASIMIR, who takes a bouquet from a servant following him. SIMBA leaves.*)

143

CASIMIR: (*Handing over his flowers.*) Allow me to congratulate you, Madam, on your triumph yesterday evening. Your debut has taken Munich by storm. But you cannot have made a more lasting impression on any of your audience than myself.

ANNA: Even if that were true, sir, I'm more than surprised to see you here in person.

CASIMIR: D'you have a moment? – I assure you, it's a purely practical matter.

ANNA: (*Invites him to sit.*) I think you may be on a false trail.

CASIMIR: (*When they've both sat.*) We shall soon see. – I wish to ask if you'd consent to be my wife.

ANNA: What am I to make of that?

CASIMIR: That's why I'm here. So we don't misunderstand each other. Allow me to make it clear from the very beginning that you will of course have to forego the enticing artistic career which opened up for you last night.

ANNA: You haven't given this a great deal of thought, have you.

CASIMIR: At my age, Madam, one does nothing without a great deal of thought. Would you like to tell me what other obstacles might stand in your way?

ANNA: You must be aware I can't answer that kind of question properly.

CASIMIR: Of course I am. But I'm speaking of the not-too-remote eventuality that you weren't able to decide your future in total freedom.

ANNA: At the moment I cannot imagine such a possibility arising.

CASIMIR: And I am currently the most highly thought of man in Munich. But tomorrow I could be sitting behind bars. I don't think badly of my best friend for asking how he stands with me in such an eventuality.

ANNA: Would you think as well of your wife if she asked the same question?

CASIMIR: My wife, certainly. My mistress never. And I don't wish to hear the answer from you now. I speak only in the event that you're let down or things transpire that sever existing ties. In a nutshell, that you don't know which way to turn.

ANNA: You'd want to make me your wife then?

CASIMIR: It may seem crazy to you. And it says a lot for your modesty. I have, as you may know, two small children at home, girls of three and six. There are other considerations, as you can imagine... As for you, I'm sure I won't be disappointed in my expectations and will assume total responsibility for the same.

ANNA: I'm amazed by your self-confidence.

CASIMIR: You can rely on me utterly. – I can tell you, I envy the creator of that Hall of Wonders his touch. And by the way, I must offer you my special compliments on your choice of costume for last night's concert. I have to admit it was all I could do to give your singing the attention it deserved.

ANNA: You mustn't believe I in any way over-estimate the applause my artistic endeavour enjoyed.

CASIMIR: I would never imagine that in you. But your teacher told me last night that success such as yours has been the undoing of many people in the past. However great the reward on a specific occasion, the truth is, such people live constantly on hand-outs.

ANNA: I was amazed how well the audience received all the performers.

CASIMIR: (*Rising.*) Except for that unfortunate symphony from Herr Samrjaki, which in time no doubt we shall come to revere as a divine artistic manifestation. Well then, we'll let the world take its course, hope for the best and be prepared for the worst. – Allow me, Madam, to take my leave.

(*He goes. ANNA holds her temples, then goes to the games room, raises the curtain and steps back.*)

ANNA: You didn't even shut the door!

HERMANN: (*Entering.*) I'd never have thought it! Not in my wildest dreams!

ANNA: You'd better go now, so he finds you at home.

HERMANN: (*Noticing the second bouquet.*) Are the flowers from him? – Seems I get it from him. – Only he didn't spend as much on his.

ANNA: Where on earth d'you get the money for such lunatic gestures?

HERMANN: (*Significantly.*) The Marquis of Keith.

ANNA: Please now, go! You've been up all night. No doubt you were carousing into the small hours?

HERMANN: I helped save Samrjaki's life.

ANNA: It's doubtless sweet of you to show sympathy for the unfortunate. But you should never sit at the same table with them. Bad luck is infectious.

HERMANN: (*Significantly.*) The Marquis of Keith told me the same thing.

ANNA: Go now. Please.

(*SIMBA comes in from the hall, with another card.*)

SIMBA: The gentleman craves your indulgence.

ANNA: (*Reading the card.*) 'The South German Concert Agency' – tell him to come back in a fortnight.

(*SIMBA goes.*)

HERMANN: What answer will you give my father?

ANNA: You are becoming a nuisance! It's high time you left.

HERMANN: I'm going to London. Even if I have to steal the money. My father will never have need to complain about me again.

ANNA: But mostly you're doing it for yourself.

HERMANN: (*Uneasy.*) I owe it to my little sisters.

(*Goes.*)

ANNA: (*Thinks a moment then calls.*) Kathi!

SIMBA: (*Entering from the dining room.*) Ma'am?

ANNA: I'm going out.

(*The doorbell sounds in the hall.*)

SIMBA: At once, Ma'am.

(*She goes to open the door. ANNA goes out to the games room. Immediately SIMBA shows in ERNST SCHOLZ. He walks with the aid of an elegant crutch, limping on his stiff knee and carrying a huge bunch of flowers.*)

SCHOLZ: This is the first opportunity I've had to thank you, dear child, for your tactful and sensitive conduct at the garden party recently.

SIMBA: (*Formal.*) Would His Lordship like me to announce him to Her Ladyship?

(*KEITH enters from the hall in a light-coloured overcoat, and with a bundle of newspapers in his hand.*)

KEITH: (*Dumping his coat.*) What a stroke of luck finding you here! (*Seeing SIMBA.*) What are you doing here?

SIMBA: Her Ladyship has taken me on as her servant.

KEITH: You see, I've made your fortune. – Announce us.

SIMBA: Very good, Herr Baron.

KEITH: This morning's papers are full of the most gushing reviews of last night's concert.

(*He sits at the table down left and flicks through the papers.*)

SCHOLZ: Have you heard where your wife's got to?

KEITH: With her parents in Buckeburg. You disappeared very quickly from the meal after the show.

SCHOLZ: I felt a keen need to be alone. How is your wife?

KEITH: Thank you for asking. Her father faces bankruptcy.

SCHOLZ: Well you'll have more than enough to save them from the worst.

KEITH: D'you know what that concert cost me last night?

SCHOLZ: You take these matters too lightly.

KEITH: I suppose you'd like me to hatch the eggs of Eternity alongside you?

SCHOLZ: I'd be more than happy for some of my excessive sense of duty to rub off on you.

KEITH: Heaven forbid! Not when I finally have the elasticity to exploit my success to the full.

SCHOLZ: (*Composed.*) I owe it to you that I can now look life levelly in the eye. Which is why I consider it my duty to speak to you as frankly as you spoke to me a fortnight ago.

KEITH: The only difference being I haven't asked for your advice.

SCHOLZ: All the more reason for the most unrestrained candour on my part. Thanks to my exaggerated sense of duty I caused the death of twenty people. But you take pleasure in gambling with the lives of others!

KEITH: Only in my case everyone so far has come out smelling of roses.

SCHOLZ: (*With increasing self-confidence.*) That's your personal good fortune. What you fail to recognise is that others have precisely the same expectation of enjoying their lives as you.

KEITH: Well at least you're consistent. You come to Munich with the express desire to turn yourself into an Epicurean, and inadvertently turn yourself into a moraliser.

SCHOLZ: I can certainly claim to have achieved a modest but nonetheless reliable self-knowledge, such that – if you would only listen – I could speak as one.

KEITH: (*Irritated.*) The truth is, my good fortune turns your blood to gall!

SCHOLZ: I don't believe in your good fortune. I'm so unspeakably happy myself I'd gladly embrace the whole world. And I honestly wish you the same. But you will never achieve it as long as you make fun of the highest values in life in that juvenile way of yours. It's true that when I came to Munich I only knew the value of the spiritual relationship between man and woman. Sensual pleasure remained something base. That was wrong. But you have never in your whole life looked for anything other than sensual pleasure from a woman.

KEITH: (*Matter of fact.*) In fact it's quite the opposite. I owe my material freedom to the past fortnight, and in consequence I can finally achieve true appreciation of life.

SCHOLZ: With one difference. The reason for all my appreciation of life is to become a useful member of society again.

KEITH: (*Jumping up.*) Why on earth should one wish to become a useful member of society!

SCHOLZ: Because as anything else you have no justification for living!

KEITH: I don't need a justification! I never asked for this life, and so I'm quite justified in living exactly as I think fit!

SCHOLZ: At the same time calmly consigning to misery the woman who has borne all the dangers and deprivations of your past three years.

KEITH: What can I do? My expenses have been so outrageous, I haven't got a penny for my own purposes. The first instalment of my salary will go on my share of the founding capital.

SCHOLZ: I can let you have ten or twenty thousand, if you can see no other way. I happened to receive a draft for ten thousand from my trustees today.
(*Takes a note from his wallet and passes it to KEITH.*)

KEITH: (*Snatching it from his hand.*) Just don't come back tomorrow saying you want it back!

SCHOLZ: I don't need it just now. – I'd have to ask my banker in Breslau to send the other ten on.
(*ANNA comes in from the games room, dressed in elegant street-clothes.*)

ANNA: I'm sorry to keep you waiting, gentlemen.

SCHOLZ: (*Handing her his flowers.*) I couldn't deny myself the pleasure, dear lady, of congratulating you with all my heart on the first morning of a career which promises so much!

ANNA: (*Putting the flowers in a vase.*) Thank you. I completely forgot in the excitement last night to ask how your injuries were.

SCHOLZ: God knows they're not worth the mention. My doctor says, in a week I could be climbing Mont Blanc if I so desired. I did however find the laughter painful with which Herr Samrjaki's symphony was greeted last night.

KEITH: (*Having sat at his desk.*) All I can do is give people the opportunity to show what they can do. There are plenty of conductors in Munich.

SCHOLZ: But didn't you yourself say he was the greatest musical genius since Wagner?

KEITH: I'd hardly call my own mount a nag. (*Rises.*)

SCHOLZ: (*To ANNA.*) No doubt Madam has important business plans she wishes to discuss with her fortunate impresario.

ANNA: No, please, we have nothing pressing to discuss. Are you thinking of leaving us?

SCHOLZ: Perhaps you'd allow me the honour to come again in a few days time?

ANNA: Be my guest. You're welcome any time.

(*SCHOLZ presses KEITH's hand briefly and goes.*)

KEITH: The morning papers are full of glowing reviews of your performance last night.

ANNA: Have you finally heard where Molly is?

KEITH: She's with her parents in Buckeburg. Tossed in an ocean of petty-bourgeois sentimentality.

ANNA: We mustn't let ourselves be so scared by her next time. All she actually wanted was to let you know how thoroughly you needed her. Even so, you really should let people into your business confidence more. Sitting on a volcano day and night can hardly be called pleasure.

KEITH: Why am I getting moral lectures from all sides today?

ANNA: Because you behave as if you needed to be permanently drunk. You give yourself no peace. I always find, the moment I'm in doubt whether to do A or B, the best thing is to do nothing at all. I've always done as little as possible and enjoyed lifelong happiness. You can't blame people for being suspicious of you, if they see you chasing fortune day and night like some starving wolf.

KEITH: It's not my fault if I'm ravenous.

ANNA: But there are people out there in sledges with rifles. The next thing you know – bang!

KEITH: I'm bullet-proof. I've still got two in me from Cuba. Besides which I possess the most impregnable guarantee of good fortune. Twenty years ago a young Trautenau and I stood in our surplices before the altar at our little village church. The village priest gave us both a little illustrated book with a saying from the bible on the front. I've hardly seen the inside of a church since, but whenever I encounter adversity, I laugh at it, remembering that saying: 'To those who love God, all things shall be granted.'

ANNA: Those who love God! You still count yourself one of those!

KEITH: I've examined every religion in existence and found in none of them the slightest difference between loving God and loving one's own well-being.

(*SIMBA comes in from the hall.*)

SIMBA: Could the Marquis step outside a moment? Sasha's here.

KEITH: Why doesn't he come in?

SASHA: (*Coming in with a telegram.*) I din't know whether I should or not cos yer said not to bring you any telegrams in public.

KEITH: (*Opens the telegram, screws it up and throws it away.*) Dammit! – My coat!

ANNA: From Molly?

KEITH: No! – I just hope to God no one finds out.

ANNA: Is she not with her parents?

KEITH: (*As SASHA helps him into his coat.*) No!

ANNA: But just now you said –

KEITH: Is it my fault she's not in Buckeburg? – The moment you think you're in clover, you find your neck's in a noose.

(*KEITH and SASHA leave. SIMBA picks up the telegram and gives it to ANNA.*)

SIMBA: The Marquis forgot his telegram.

ANNA: Bring me my hat.

(*The doorbell rings in the hall.*)

SIMBA: At once, M'm.

(*Goes to open the door.*)

ANNA: (*Reading the telegram.*) 'Molly not with us. Please inform of her whereabouts by return. Yours anxiously.'

SIMBA: (*Returning.*) The Herr Baron forgot his gloves.

ANNA: Which Herr Baron?

SIMBA: The bon viveur.

ANNA: (*Hunting around.*) Mary and Joseph, where are
　　they...?

SCHOLZ: (*Entering.*) If Madam will permit me a few words
　　more.

ANNA: I'm just going out. (*To SIMBA.*) My hat – quickly.
　　(*SIMBA goes.*)

SCHOLZ: My friend being here prevented me speaking
　　openly...

ANNA: Could this wait for a more suitable opportunity?

SCHOLZ: I'd intended waiting a little longer to hear from
　　you. But my feelings force my hand, Madam. To leave
　　you in no doubt that my proposition is concerned only
　　with your happiness, allow me to confess that I am –
　　unspeakably – in love with you.

ANNA: And what is your proposition?

SCHOLZ: No doubt many obstacles will stand in your way
　　before you can enjoy the full fruit of unqualified
　　recognition...

ANNA: I'm aware of that, but I have no intention of ever
　　singing again.

SCHOLZ: Not singing? How many would give their lives
　　for your gifts!

ANNA: Is that all you've got to tell me?

SCHOLZ: I can see I've unwittingly offended you again.
　　You naturally expected me to offer you my hand –

ANNA: Isn't that what you were after?

SCHOLZ: I wanted to ask you to be my lover. – I couldn't
　　honour you any more greatly than I would as my wife.
　　(*From this point he speaks with the reckless, lungeing gestures
　　of a madman.*) Be it lover or wife, I offer you my life,
　　everything I own...

ANNA: I thought you wanted to become a useful member
　　of society.

SCHOLZ: I dreamed of making the world happy, as a
　　prisoner behind bars dreams of infinite glaciers! Now I
　　wish for one thing only. Making the woman I love so
　　unspeakably happy she never regrets her choice.

ANNA: I'm sorry to have to tell you I don't care for you.

SCHOLZ: Don't care for me! I've never enjoyed so many proofs of affection as from you!

ANNA: I'm not to blame for that. Your friend described you to me as a philosopher who cares nothing for the real world.

SCHOLZ: But the real world has relieved me of my philosophy!

ANNA: The Marquis of Keith finds his confirmation text helps him over his misfortunes. He looks on it as an infallible magic spell, at which police and bailiffs will run a mile.

SCHOLZ: I would not debase myself so far as to believe in prophecy. But were that soldier of fortune to be correct, then I received at my confirmation an equally inviolable recipe for unhappiness. The pastor gave me at that time the saying 'Many are called, but few are chosen'.

ANNA: Surely the person to complain to is the Marquis?

SCHOLZ: But I'm not complaining! The longer this school of hard knocks goes on, the more tempered is one's faculty to resist it spiritually. My soul is indestructible.

ANNA: Then I congratulate you.

SCHOLZ: And that's why I cannot he resisted! The less you feel for me, the greater and mightier my love for you becomes, the nearer comes that moment when you say I fought you with all the powers at my disposal, but I love you!

ANNA: Heaven forbid!

SCHOLZ: Heaven can't! When a man of my willpower concentrates all his effort and power towards one goal, there can only be two possible outcomes: he achieves his end, or he loses his wits.

ANNA: You may well he right.

SCHOLZ: And I'm ready to take that risk! I anticipate the worst, but refuse to look back till I've reached my goal. If I can't make a life for myself from the ecstasy of the moment, then there's no hope for me. The opportunity will never come again!

ANNA: Thank you so much for reminding me. (*She sits at her writing desk.*)

SCHOLZ: I see the world before me in all its glory for the last time!

ANNA: (*Writing a note.*) That applies to me too. (*Calls.*) Kathi! (*To herself.*) I shall never have this opportunity again either.

SCHOLZ: (*Suddenly coming to his senses.*) What are you thinking, Madam? What do you suspect? You're wrong, Madam. Please don't imagine for a moment –

ANNA: Have you still not realised you're keeping me? (*Calls.*) Kathi!

SCHOLZ: I can't leave you like this. You must reassure me you don't fear for my sanity.

(*SIMBA enters with ANNA's hat.*)

ANNA: Where've you been all this time?

SIMBA: I didn't dare come in.

SCHOLZ: Simba, you above all must know I have my wits about me.

SIMBA: (*Pushing him away.*) Stop it! Don't be so daft!

ANNA: Kindly leave my maid be. (*To SIMBA.*) D'you know Consul Casimir's address?

SCHOLZ: (*As if suddenly turned to stone.*) I bear the mark of Cain upon my brow...

End of Act Four

ACT FIVE

The Marquis of Keith's study. Doors stand wide open. As HERMANN CASIMIR sits at the central table, KEITH calls into the living room.

KEITH: Sasha! (*Getting no answer, he goes towards the anteroom. To HERMANN.*) Excuse me. (*Calls into the anteroom.*) Sasha! (*Comes downstage, to HERMANN.*) So you're off to London, and with your father's permission. I can give you some good advice about London. (*Throws himself on the divan.*) First of all, I strongly recommend you leave your German sentimentality at home. Social democracy and anarchism cut no ice whatsoever in London any more. And another thing: the only real way to get the most out of your fellow-man is to play on their best qualities. Therein lies the art of being loved and being right. The more indulgently you judge your fellow-man, the more scrupulously they have to work to keep right on their side. And − my main pearl of wisdom − the most dazzling business in this world is morality. I have not yet reached a level where I can pursue this business, but I wouldn't be the Marquis of Keith if I let it slip through my fingers. (*The bell rings in the hall. He calls.*) Sasha! (*Rising.*) That boy'll get a clipped ear. (*He goes into the hall and comes back with Herr OSTERMEIER.*) You couldn't have come at a more opportune moment, Herr Ostermeier...

OSTERMEIER: My dear friend, my colleagues on t' board have delegated me −

KEITH: I want to discuss a plan with you which will increase our income several times over.

OSTERMEIER: D'you really want me to stand up at our next general meeting and declare that once again I have been unable to inspect your books?

KEITH: You're imagining things, my dear Herr Ostermeier! − Why don't you tell me calmly and plainly what it is you need.

OSTERMEIER: Your books, my dear friend.

KEITH: (*Flaring up.*) I run myself ragged for those bleary-
eyed blockheads...

OSTERMEIER: So he was right! (*Turning to go.*) My
compliments, sir...

KEITH: (*Tears the desk-drawer open.*) Here, help yourself.
Wallow in account books. (*Turning back to
OSTERMEIER.*) Who was right?

OSTERMEIER: A certain Herr Raspe, Commissioner of
Police who, last night in the *Bar Americaine,* bet five
bottles of Pommery you kept no account books.

KEITH: (*Bridling.*) Nor do I.

OSTERMEIER: Then show me your copy-book.

KEITH: When am I supposed to have had the time since
the company was founded to set up an office!

OSTERMEIER: Just show me your copy-book.

KEITH: (*Bridling again.*) I have none.

OSTERMEIER: Then show me your deposit slips from th'
bank.

KEITH: Did I take what you gave me to leave it gathering
interest?

OSTERMEIER: My dear friend, there's no need to excite
yourself. Even if you keep no books, you must make a
note of your outgoings somewhere. Even messenger boys
do that.

KEITH: (*Throws his notebook on the table.*) There. My
notebook.

OSTERMEIER: (*Opens it and reads.*) 'A flood of silver in
paillettes and pale violet silk from shoulder to ankle.' –
This is it?

KEITH: If all you can do, after I've achieved success upon
success, is throw obstacles in my path, then you count on
one thing for certain: you'll never see your money again
– in this world or the next.

OSTERMEIER: The share price is not that bad, my friend.
We'll see our money all right. – My compliments.
(*Turns to go.*)

KEITH: (*Holding him back.*) All this ferreting about will
undermine the entire operation. – You must forgive me,

sir. I get excited because I feel towards our Hall of
Wonders rather like a father towards his child.

OSTERMEIER: Then you need fear for your child no
more, sir. The Hall of Wonders is underwritten and will
be built.

KEITH: Without me?

OSTERMEIER: If necessary, without you, my friend.

KEITH: You can't do this!

OSTERMEIER: I might add, you're the last person who
can stop us.

KEITH: It would be a move of scurrilous infamy!

OSTERMEIER: That's rich indeed! Because we refuse to
let ourselves be cheated by you any longer, you call us
cheats!

KEITH: If you think you're being cheated, take me to court
and try to get your money back.

OSTERMEIER: That's all very well sir, but we're on th'
board.

KEITH: You're on the board to support me in my work!

OSTERMEIER: And that's why I'm here. But there's nowt
to work on.

KEITH: My dear Herr Ostermeier, you cannot ask me, a
man of honour, to put up with such baseness. You take
the business side over. Let me remain simply its artistic
director. I'll admit I've been incorrect in my handling of
the business, but I condoned it in myself only in the
knowledge that it was happening for the last time, and
that, as soon as my circumstances were assured, I would
never let myself be put in that position again.

OSTERMEIER: We might've spoken about this yesterday,
when th' other gentlemen were here. But instead you
jawed t' hind leg off a donkey. I'd even say to you today,
let's give it another chance – if you could at least have
shown yourself to be an honest man. But if all one hears
is untruths…

KEITH: (*Bridling.*) Then tell the gentlemen this. I will build
my Hall of Wonders just as surely as the idea for it came
from my head. But you try and build it – tell them this –

and I'll blow the whole thing sky-high, board, shareholders, the lot!

OSTERMEIER: I will do that immediately, sir. After all I'd hate anyone to receive this as a smack in the face, let alone... Your servant.

(*He goes.*)

KEITH: (*Staring after him.*) A smack on the arse. That's how it feels. (*To HERMANN.*) Don't leave me now, or I'll shrivel up so small, I'll be afraid there's nothing left of me. – How can this happen? (*With tears in his eyes.*) After all the fireworks! – Am I to be hounded from country to country again like an outlaw? – No! I will not go to the wall! (*Drawing himself to his full height.*) No, I will astound all Munich with my panache. If he goes on shaking the tree, I shall fall straight on his head with the greatest possible hullabaloo, scattering them in all directions and smashing them to little pieces. And we shall see who gets back on his feet again first.

(*Countess WERDENFELS enters.*)

KEITH: (*Rushing towards her.*) My queen!

ANNA: (*To HERMANN.*) Would you leave us a moment?

KEITH: (*Shutting the door behind him.*) You look very preoccupied.

ANNA: That's quite possible. Every day since our concert I've received a half dozen offers of marriage.

KEITH: What the hell do I care!

ANNA: But I do.

KEITH: (*Sarcastic.*) Have you fallen in love with him then?

ANNA: Who d'you mean?

KEITH: Our bon viveur.

ANNA: You're making fun of me.

KEITH: Who are you talking about then?

ANNA: (*Pointing to the living room.*) His father.

KEITH: And this is what you want to talk to me about?

ANNA: No, I wanted to ask if you'd finally had any word from Molly.

KEITH: No – but what's all this about Casimir?

ANNA: What's this about Molly!! – Are you keeping her disappearance a secret?

KEITH: (*Anxious.*) If I'm frank, I'm less afraid something's happened to her than that her disappearance will pull the rug from under my feet. And if that shows no humanity, the other side is, I've sat in the telegraph office all night for the past three nights. – My crime against her is, in all the time we've known each other, she's never had a cross word from me. She's gnawed with longing for her narrow little world where, shoulder to shoulder, you knuckle down and graft and love each other. No vision, no room to breathe, nothing but love! As much as possible and of the most ordinary kind!

ANNA: And what happens if she isn't found?

KEITH: Rest assured, when my roof has fallen about my ears, I can count on her coming back, smiling ruefully and saying 'I'm not going through that again'. – Her goal has been reached. I can pack my bags.

ANNA: And what'll become of me?

KEITH: So far you've done better than anyone from our little enterprise, and I hope you'll do even better. You can't lose anything because you've got nothing at stake in it.

ANNA: Are you sure of that?

KEITH: Ah, I see.

ANNA: Yes, exactly.

KEITH: What answer did you give him?

ANNA: I wrote and told him I couldn't give him an answer at present.

KEITH: You wrote him that!

ANNA: I wanted to speak to you first.

KEITH: (*Grabs her by the wrist and throws her from him.*) If all I mean to you is that you need to speak to me, then...go ahead, marry him!

ANNA: Anyone who holds feelings in the contempt you do should be able to talk calmly about purely practical matters.

KEITH: My feelings don't come into this! What infuriates me is that you have so little pride in your blood you're prepared to sell your first-born for a mess of pottage!

ANNA: A mess of portage being anything but you.

KEITH: I know my weaknesses. But these people are... puppydogs! If they're not short on grey matter, they're short on backbone! D'you want to bring mongrels into the world who don't open their eyes for the first week? I'd happily let you go off on your career if I and all the passion I've breathed into you have really had it. But if you bury yourself away from your destiny as an artist beneath some moneybags, you're worth no more than the grass growing out of the grave!

ANNA: If the least you had was a clue about what's happened to Molly!

KEITH: Don't insult me! (*Calls.*) Sasha!

ANNA: If you absolutely insist on our going our separate ways –

KEITH: Absolutely, I do.

ANNA: – then I'll have my letters back.

KEITH: (*Sarcastic.*) Why, are you writing your memoirs?

ANNA: No, but they might get into the wrong hands.

KEITH: (*Jumping up.*) Sasha!

ANNA: What d'you want Sasha for? I sent him on an errand.

KEITH: How come?

ANNA: He came to me. I've done it several times before. If the worst comes to the worst, at least the boy knows where he can earn a few shillings.

KEITH: (*Falls into the armchair by his desk.*) My Sasha! (*Wipes the tears from his eyes.*) You even think of him! – If you leave the room now, Anna, I'll just buckle, like an ox in the slaughterhouse. – Just give me a few days' grace.

ANNA: I can't afford to waste time.

KEITH: Just so I get used to the idea, Anna. I need my wits about me now more than ever...

ANNA: Will you give me my letters back?

KEITH: You're a monster! – But that's your enlightened form of pity, I suppose. At least then I can curse you when you're no longer mine.

ANNA: As long as you live, you will never learn to judge women properly.

KEITH: (*Pulling himself up proudly.*) I'll never recant my beliefs, not even on the rack. You follow fortune – that's only human. So what you were to me, you remain.

ANNA: Then give me my letters.

KEITH: No, my dear child. I'm keeping your letters for myself. Otherwise, on my death-bed I'll be wondering if you weren't just a mirage I had. (*Kisses her hand.*) Good luck!

ANNA: Even without you.

(*She goes.*)

KEITH: (*Alone, he doubles up with a heart-spasm.*) Ah! Ah! I'm dying! (*He rushes to the desk, takes a handful of letters from the drawer and hurries to the door.*) Anna! Anna! (*Coming through the open door, ERNST SCHOLZ meets him. He walks without hindrance, no sign of his injury visible.*) (*Recoiling.*) I was just coming to your hotel.

SCHOLZ: There's no point. I'm leaving.

KEITH: In that case give me the twenty thousand marks you promised me yesterday.

SCHOLZ: I'm not giving you any more money.

KEITH: The caryatids are smashing me to pieces! They're trying to take my directorship away!

SCHOLZ: That only reinforces my decision.

KEITH: It's just getting over this temporary crisis!

SCHOLZ: My money's worth more than you. My money will secure for my family a free, exalted, pre-eminence for generations to come. While you will never do anyone any good whatsoever!

KEITH: Where does a worthless heap like you get the neck to call me useless!

SCHOLZ: Let's forget our rivalry. – I've finally achieved the great sacrifice which so many in this world must bring themselves to at least once.

KEITH: And that is?

SCHOLZ: I've freed myself from my illusions.

KEITH: (*Sarcastic.*) Are you wallowing in love for another low-class girl?

SCHOLZ: I've freed myself from everything. – I've admitted myself to a private clinic.

KEITH: (*Yelling.*) There's nothing more contemptible, more shameful you can do to your self than betray it!

SCHOLZ: I understand your outrage very well. In the past three days I've gone through the most awful struggle that could befall even the poorest earthworm.

KEITH: In order to creep away like a coward? – To come out and triumphantly renounce your human dignity?

SCHOLZ: (*Bridling.*) I'm not renouncing my dignity! You have cause neither to insult, nor to mock me. Anyone who's looked reality straight in the face as I have, cannot possibly forfeit either the respect or the sympathy of his fellow-man.

KEITH: (*Shrugs.*) I'd think it over if I was you.

SCHOLZ: I've given it plenty of thought. It's the last remaining duty my fate requires me to fulfil.

KEITH: Once you're in, you know, it's not so easy to get out.

SCHOLZ: If I had even the slightest hope of coming out, I wouldn't go in the first place. I now no longer have the slightest doubt that I'm quite different from the rest of mankind.

KEITH: (*With great pride.*) Thankfully, I've never had the same doubt.

SCHOLZ: (*Very calm.*) I always took you for the greatest of swindlers. Now I've even given up that illusion. Swindlers always have luck. Just as an honest man, even if his luck never changes, at least keeps his good conscience. Your luck is no better than mine, and you don't know it. And that's the awful menace hanging over you.

KEITH: There's no greater menace hanging over me than waking up broke tomorrow!

SCHOLZ: You'll never be anything else. I'd like to think you were safe from the awful consequences of your blindness. Which is why I've come to see you one last time. I'm honestly convinced the best thing you can do is come with me.

KEITH: (*Waiting for it.*) Where?

SCHOLZ: To the clinic.

KEITH: Give me thirty thousand marks and I'll be there!

SCHOLZ: If you come with me, you won't need any money.
You'll fmd it a more comfortable home than any you've
known. We'll go riding, play billiards –

KEITH: (*Clutching him.*) Give me the thirty thousand marks!
D'you want me to go down on my knees? I could be
leaving this place under police escort!

SCHOLZ: It's gone that far already? (*Pushing him back.*) I
wouldn't give money like that to a madman.

KEITH: (*Screams.*) You're the madman!

SCHOLZ: (*Calm.*) I've come completely to my senses.

KEITH: (*Sarcastic.*) If you want to have yourself committed
because you've come to your senses, then off you go!

SCHOLZ: You're the kind they have to drag in screaming!

KEITH: (*Venomous.*) If you consider it your moral duty to
free the world of your superfluous presence, you can find
a more radical solution than riding and billiards!

SCHOLZ: I tried that long ago.

KEITH: (*Yelling at him.*) Then what are you doing still here!

SCHOLZ: (*Darkly.*) It didn't work. Like everything else.

KEITH: I suppose you shot someone else by mistake!

SCHOLZ: They cut the bullets out from between my
shoulder blades, next to the backbone. – No doubt today
is the last time in your life anyone will offer to save you.
You know yourself what you have to look forward to.

KEITH: (*Falls to his knees and clutches SCHOLZ's hands.*)
Give me the forty thousand and I'll be saved!

SCHOLZ: It won't save you from prison.

KEITH: (*Jumping up, aghast.*) Shut up!

SCHOLZ: (*Pleading.*) Come with me and you'll be safe. We
grew up together. I don't see why we can't see the end
through together as well. Society will condemn you as a
criminal and subject you to all kinds of inhuman,
medieval torture…

KEITH: (*Wailing.*) If you can't help me, then go, I beg you!

SCHOLZ: Come now. – It would be a faint gleam of light
in the evening of my days to know the friend of my

youth has been snatched from the awful fate which awaits
him.

KEITH: Go! Please!

SCHOLZ: Entrust yourself to my care, as I entrusted myself
to you...

KEITH: (*A desperate scream.*) Sasha! Sasha!

SCHOLZ: Then don't forget where you have a friend with
whom you'll be welcome any time.
(*Goes.*)

KEITH: (*Crawls around, looking for something.*) Molly! Molly!
For the first time in my life I'm on my knees to a
woman. (*Suddenly listens to a sound in the living room.*)
There...there! (*Having opened the living room door.*) Ah, it's
you. (*HERMANN CASIMIR comes in from the living room.*)
I can't ask you to stay long. I'm not...at my best. I
need...tonight to sleep on it, to get on top of things
again. – Go with...with... (*Heavy footsteps and several voices
are heard from the landing.*) D'you hear? What a noise!
Uproar! I fear the worst...

HERMANN: Shut your door.

KEITH: I can't. I can't! It's her.
(*A number of regulars from the Hofbrauhaus drag in
MOLLY's dead body. She drips with water, her clothes hang
in tatters. Her hair has come loose and covers her face.*)

BUTCHER'S BOY: There 'e is, the ponce! (*Talking over his
shoulder.*) Got her? (*To KEITH.*) See what us caught? Have
a look if tha can face it!

PORTER: Fished it out t' river. Caught up in t' ironwork
gates. Musta been in th' water a week.

BAKER'S WIFE: An' all the while the dirty bugger's
parading arm-in-arm wi' 'is shameless hussies. Six weeks
since 'e last paid for 'is bread. Lets 'is poor wife go round
all t' shops beggin' for summat to eat. A stone woulda
wept to see th' way she were lookin' at th' last!

KEITH: (*Retreats to his desk as the crowd presses round him with
the corpse.*) Please, just calm yourselves!

BUTCHER'S BOY: Shut yer gob, you damn con-man. Or
ah'll smack yer so hard yer won't get up. – Have a look.
– Is it her or in't it? – Look, damn yer.

KEITH: (*Behind his back has picked up HERMANN's revolver, left there by Countess WERDENFELS earlier.*) Take your hands off me, unless you want me to use this!

BUTCHER'S BOY: What's he say, the cream puff? – What was that!! – Gimme that gun. In't that one there enough for yer, yer bastard? – Gimme it!

(*He wrestles with KEITH, who succeeds in edging towards the exit, just as CONSUL CASIMIR comes in. HERMANN CASIMIR meanwhile has pressed forward to the corpse, which he and the BAKER'S WIFE carry to the divan.*)

KEITH: (*Resisting desperately, calls out.*) Police! Police! (*Sees CASIMIR and clutches hold of him.*) Help me, for God's sake. I'm being lynched!

CASIMIR: (*To the people.*) Come on now, be off wi' yer, or yer'll see my other side. – Leave the woman there! – Quick march, I said! – That's where t' carpenter left th' hole! (*Taking his son, who tries to leave with the crowd, by the arm.*) Hold it, pal! You can tek a lesson to London wi' yer. (*The Hofbrauhaus regulars have left the room. To KEITH.*) I were going to ask you to leave Munich in th' next twenty-four hours. Now I'm thinking it'd be best for you if you left on th' next train.

KEITH: (*Still holding the revolver in his left hand.*) I'm not responsible for this...misfortune.

CASIMIR: That's a matter for your conscience. But you are responsible for forging my signature on a telegram at your launch party in the Brienner Strasse.

KEITH: I can't travel just now...

CASIMIR: (*Hands him a paper.*) Perhaps you'd sign this receipt. It's to certify you've received a sum of ten thousand marks owed to you by the Countess Werdenfels, which you've received back from me. (*KEITH goes to the desk and signs. CASIMIR counts the money from his wallet.*) As your successor in the Directorship of the Hall of Wonders Company I'd urge you, in the interests of a successful outcome to our enterprise, not to be seen m Munich again. (*Standing by his desk, KEITH gives CASIMIR the paper and receives the*

money mechanically. CASIMIR pockets the paper.) Safe journey! (*To HERMANN.*) Quick march, you!
(*HERMANN slips out shyly. CASIMIR follows him.*)

KEITH: (*The revolver in his left hand, the money in his right, takes a few steps towards the sofa but sways back in horror. Then he looks indecisively at the revolver and the money alternately...and, leaving the revolver on the central table behind him, he grins.*) One minute up, the next down...

The End.